MARIA PAVIOUR

Changing

Vampires

Into

ANGELS

SIX STEPS TO HEAVEN
IN YOUR RELATIONSHIPS

Illustrated by Cole Paviour

Isiliver Books
Read your way to a better world

Isiliver Books
Published by Isiliver Books UK
Isiliver Books, Michel Delving House,
Hadlow Down, East Sussex, England TN22 4HS

British Library Cataloguing in Publication Data

ISBN 0-9543654-0-2

Printed and bound in United Kingdom by
Pro-Print, Carmarthen, Wales
Set in Arial Narrow and Baskerville Old Face

First Edition
Printed in the UK 2002

Contents

Dedication

For Stuart who has taught me the most about relationships and my parents for giving me a good start in life.

About the Author

Maria Paviour studied psychology and education at London University and graduated in 1985 with an excellent degree and a First Class newborn baby! Much to Maria and Stuart Paviour's delight their family has increased, with one child per decade, and they now have Tate (born 1994) and Jasmin (born 2000) to join Cole (born 1985).

Maria's career in personal development has spanned 15 years, working in organisations, including large corporations, as training and development manager, company director and finally in her current role as a consultant.

Maria and Stuart set up Synergy Training ten years ago specialising in communication and relationships. Maria's expertise in learning and personal development has led to her being invited to work extensively with large corporate clients as well as individuals in the UK and Africa. Maria now trains independent consultants to use the unique Synergy approach to learning.

Maria's psychological research has spearheaded the development of a unique system for monitoring and "treating" poor well-being in companies with the Well Being @ Work programme.

Nearly 9 years ago Maria began her first studies of the Vampires and Angels concept and she runs workshops that focus on helping people to "banish the vampire and awaken the angel" within themselves and their relationships. She has received many accolades from her clients as to the efficacy of these methods.

Maria and Stuart's philosophy of valuing both career and family life proves that relationships can thrive when partners live and work together.

Foreword:

I first learned about vampires at the start of the new Millennium when I was lucky enough to attend one of Maria's workshops in Milton Keynes. The students that day ranged from high level professionals working for multinational corporations to Reiki healers and all were initially intrigued, and ultimately, convinced in what she had to say.

Maria told us about Vampires. You could see everyone's minds working furiously to imagine all the incidents in their own lives when they had been bitten by Vampires, or worse still, when they had been vampiric themselves. But that's the beauty of the vampire theory. It is much more than a metaphor for we can all recall, with little difficulty the people who have drained us not of blood, but of energy. We have all experienced those lengthy telephone calls with the people we think of as friends, that leave us unable to get a word in edgeways, and quite deflated afterwards. We all know a Vampire.

Maria's extensive research into the modern day vampires in our midst has now been appropriately combined with the study of their antithesis and antidote. For while the first part of the book looks at vampires, the second part concentrates on angels. Here we learn how to unearth and release the angel within ourselves and lead a rewarding life filled with light and love.

Again, it is the simplicity of these theories that make them both accessible and understandable. Maria illustrates her ideas with anecdotes, examples and stories we recognise from life, fiction and film. Through the recognisable metaphors of light and dark, the mirror and the crucifix, she helps us all to understand the truth behind the myth.

Importantly, the author takes contemporary dilemmas such as stress, burnout, fatigue and insomnia and shows how vampires may be to blame. Crucially, she teaches how to recognise them and, ultimately, destroy them.

Jo Parfitt
Journalist, speaker and careers consultant
www.career-in-your-suitcase.com

Introduction
How to make better relationships

This programme will help you to change your relationships so that they become rewarding and satisfying. If you let it, this book can change your life!

Understanding Vampires:

If you have ever felt drained of energy by a relationship or after a conversation with someone then perhaps you already know an energy vampire.

There are many ways by which your energy can be stolen, and at the time it may feel quite pleasant; for example, you may have been supporting a needy friend, or simply overwhelmed by charisma; however, it may be later that you feel dissatisfied. On the other hand, you may have been bullied, or manipulated by guilt. Then again, there may be times when you have been tempted into doing something that you knew to be wrong, or have been flattened by someone who will not stop talking and talking, giving you endless advice on how you should live your life.

All these different examples have two things in common; firstly, that the interaction is dissatisfying, and secondly, that it involved a vampire. Vampires are real, but they suck your energy, not your blood, and this can be just as destructive.

For example, your boss may 'vampirise' you by stealing your ideas and failing to give you the credit, while all the time undermining your feeling of security, so that you doubt you have the ability to find another job, although you detest the one you have!

If your friends are manipulative, or cruel (even though they say "I'm only joking"!), they are probably vampirising you; or if your partner tries to change you, and is critical, these are examples of vampirism.

Why do vampires steal energy?

Vampires crave immediate fixes of energy. After claiming a victim the vampire will feel loved - though only temporarily; it will feel important - although insecure; it will feel powerful - although this power is dissatisfying, as it comes at the expense of intimacy, spontaneity and compassion.

The one four letter word to be feared

When I make presentations to conferences about the problem of vampirism and how it manifests itself in business I find that there is one four letter word that cannot be uttered. The word that business people find most offensive. And I apologise if this offends the reader. What is the word? It is LOVE.

Love, the only four letter word that cannot be used in the boardroom without causing a stir. What kind of world is this, I wonder, when we blanch at this?

What does the word suggest to you? What is support if not love? What is care if not love? What is compassion, if not love?

This book is not about sexuality; love is a part of us, however we express ourselves sexually. This book is about finding love within and on the outside. It is about the way in which the fear of love creates the vampire; which is precisely the reason why vampires are able to thrive in organisations where Love is considered a "dirty word".

Why do people vampirise others?

Vampires are afraid to love. They are afraid that they may be rejected, they are afraid that they are not truly worthy of being loved. They choose the power of the vampire over the love of the angel.

According to A Course In Miracles everything is either "love or a call for love". When we begin to analyse our relationships in this way we can see that the things we do are usually an attempt to gain acceptance and love from others, and that our partners, friends, colleagues are no different from us. Throughout this book you may want to ask yourself "Is this love? Or is this a call for love?" as you analyse your own behaviours and ask yourself if you are being a vampire from time to time.

How angels energise us:

Angels help us shine. We know when we have come across one, because we feel inspired, energised and loved. Interestingly, angels are able to evoke a sense of love within us. We do not turn our focus upon the angel itself, but instead upon ourselves. In other words, we notice the good things within us, we feel valued and good about whom we are.

Wouldn't it be lovely if all our relationships created that feeling? Of course they can, but to create an angel, we need to understand that both the vampires and the angels come from within ourselves. The vampires that are "out there" preying upon us are also within. Until we recognise this we cannot escape from the clutches of vampirism.

Finding the inner angel:

We are all angels on the inside and we can all become vampires. No matter how deeply entrenched a person may be in vampirism, they can always be saved. No one is beyond help; however, we need to save ourselves. We have to decide to turn our backs on the life of vampirism, and that is difficult, because it is so addictive.

When we awaken the angel that is within us we can change our lives. We consequently find our world is full of positive, supportive relationships and achievement.

In order to create angelic relationships, first we need to banish the vampires. This involves recognising the vampires who stalk us and denying them access. This is easier done than is often imagined, because when we refuse a vampire access to our energy it is enough to thwart it in these efforts! It can really be that simple. Becoming aware of vampirism often curtails it immediately.

Before trying to prevent a vampire attacking you from the outside, we need to shine the light upon the inner vampire and awaken the inner angel.

It is easier to recognise vampires than angels:

As you learn more about vampires it is very likely that you will notice them in every aspect of your life. Wherever you go you will be "vampire-spotting"; everyone you meet will appear to demonstrate some aspect of the vampire, and you may feel as though you are walking with the undead.

Where are all the angels? They are here. The reason you do not see them is simple. You will see what you are, and you may discover that you are already allowing your vampire to 'rise from the grave' and as you may know, a vampire cannot see itself in the mirror. If you are noticing vampires it is because you are in "separation". In other words, you are creating a distinction between yourself and the rest of the universe.

Connectedness

There is no separation between people and the world. We are one with all of nature, the planet and the people who live upon it. This idea that we are all bound together in some invisible way has long been a part of many religious ideologies, and is now also a part of scientific thought.

Modern physicists have now come to an agreement about the universe, and have determined that there are eleven dimensions; we know about three dimensions, depth, width and height. Einstein introduced a fourth dimension; time. Now seven more have been discovered! Confused? Well, don't worry, because only one of these dimensions is highly significant to us; that is, the eleventh dimension, which is some trillionths of a millimetre thick, but infinitely long; it is apparently like a long thread that binds every part of the universe together, unifying it.

The idea that we are all connected can be looked upon as 'unity'. For once, quantum scientists agree about the eleventh dimension, perhaps this is also unity in action!

Seeing Angels:

The irony is, that we can only see the angel within others and ourselves when we can see our vampire. We need to go through the process of driving a metaphorical stake into our own hearts, in order to discover the inner beauty and peacefulness of the angel.

Shadows cannot exist without the light, and in the same way vampires and angels are inextricably linked, we cannot have one without the other. We are all something of the vampire and the angel, or to paraphrase Kant, man walks a path between angel and beast. When we can accept the vampire and the angel within us, we can find a way to walk a path that creates better balance in our life.

The Steps to Better Relationships:

Changing Vampires into Angels will allow you to find and activate your inner cherub. It will help you to release the vampire and banish it from your life. You will discover your joy, your potential and limitless passion and energy.

The steps in this book you will enable you to:

- Banish the Inner Vampire and find contentment in your relationships
- Rid yourself of people who are draining you
- Rediscover the Inner Angel and find energy and joy within

Part One—Banishing Vampires:

In this part of the book we discover how to recognise and deal with vampires that drain us of our energy, and discover that we are probably vampires ourselves.

Many of us feel victimised by vampires, the people who drain our energy. We find them at work, at home and in our social lives. We can feel exhausted by these vampires, as they seem to seek us out, but before we can ward them off we need to examine some truths about ourselves. Perhaps we are encouraging our own vampire to rise from the grave?

The process of awakening our inner angel requires us to look within and see to this. When we feel we are being victimised by a vampire who is not present, then we know we have taken that vampire and recreated it in our minds. At this point we are vampirising ourselves with our endless thoughts and obsessing.

For example, Indira felt her boyfriend had been a vampire, she ended the relationship and no longer saw him, but thoughts about the way she had been treated kept resurfacing. Eventually she realised that she was allowing the vampire in her ex-boyfriend to victimise her, even though it existed as nothing more than thoughts and memories. Indira realised she was vampirising herself and had to face this inner vampire. This was a little scary, until she realised that the vampire was just a thought, and that thoughts could change.

By allowing ourselves to be victims of vampires, we become vampires ourselves, seeking the energy of others in order to replenish ourselves. In order to escape this dark life and move into the realm of the angels we must pull the mask off the vampire that lives inside us, within our subconscious, because underneath is our cherub, our little perfect child, hiding behind fear.

All vampires are really innocent children that are using foul means to achieve a simple aim: to be loved. These inner vampires believe themselves to be unlovable, which creates an endless circle of dissatisfaction and misery. This may continue until they can love,. cherish and nurture their inner cherub and allow it to reach its full heights of angelic potential.

This part of the book provides an insight into the processes that occur within our relationships and us. It contains the vital knowledge that we need in order to begin making changes in our lives.

Part Two—Awakening the Angel:

In the second part of the book we discover how to awaken the angel within, we find out that we have limitless energy available to us, and that we can join with others to create satisfying and energising relationships.

When we are ready to awaken our angels, we can work through the six easy steps that will take us to a lifetime of satisfactory and loving relationships, in every part of our life.

This process involves discovering and using energy that you may not have consciously had access to before. You will learn how to activate this energy within you and consequently attract positive people into your life, creating for yourself a new life of confidence and joy.

We may be able to recognise the vampire in others very easily, but when we see it within ourselves we know we have come home to a truth that will enable us to elevate our relationships to angelic status .

Chapter 1

What are Energy Vampires?

Discover:
The truth behind the vampire myth.
Why vampires steal your energy.
How to recognise a vampire.

The Truth Behind the Vampire Myth:

Vampires are real, they are out there, and they are sapping your energy.

Why vampires seem real:
It is amazing how many of us know about vampires in some detail. We have seen the films and read the books. Vampire images, concepts and mythology are enduring.

We know how vampires live, we understand their habits, what they fear and how to destroy them. All this, and yet the creature is said to inhabit only fiction. The truth is, we know that this is not the case. These stories are enduring because they resonate so strongly with us. We recognise them as real.

The fascination with vampires:
Energy Vampires are ordinary people. They do not appear to be different from us. However, these vampires are not after our blood. They are after our life force, our energy.

The myths, legends and stories we read and see in films represent well the truth of energy vampires in our world today. We now need to recognize the vampire, both within and without, in order to prevent ourselves from falling prey to vampirism, and prevent ourselves allowing our own vampire to rise from the grave and ruin our relationships.

For hundreds of years stories of vampires have featured in fairy tales and myths, and continue to endure even today. When many other "horror" stories have lost their power to terrify, it seems the vampire is still able to evoke compelling feelings of fear. We find the vampire at once repellent, repulsive and yet attractive and compulsive.

We partly fear the vampire, and yet fantasise about the vampire's sex appeal and allure. The process of vampirism is highly erotic, of all story book beasts it is the only one whose method of destroying its victim actually looks pleasant and appealing.

The most famous of all vampire stories, that of Dracula, has, interestingly, been distorted in film adaptations from Bram Stoker's original novel. In the novel Dracula was a foul looking creature, and in the latest Kenneth Brannagh film Dracula's appearance changed from ugly to beautiful. The Dracula we see is debonair and attractive with great sexual magnetism, even though we know he is evil.

Children are equally fascinated by vampires, and there are numerous children's books about them, notably Mona the Vampire and The Little Vampire. The latter was made into a film, where, interestingly, the story revolves around the vampires' desire to become free of their bondage to bloodlust.

If we describe a person as a "vampire" people immediately know what we mean because subconsciously we can relate to vampirism as a metaphor. We never seem to tire of stories about vampires because we can relate to them in our own lives.

When people are first introduced to the concept of energy vampirism their initial response is usually to go into a sense of realization, immediately recognizing the many times they have been victims, quickly able to point out vampires they have known.

Allowing our vampire to rise from the grave:

As well as being preyed upon by these energy suckers, we are just as likely to allow our own inner vampire to "rise from the grave" and suck the energy from others. The shocking thing about vampirism is that we are so frequently unaware that we have become one; we activate our vampire and then walk in the shadows seeking our next meal ticket, without any realisation that we have become a monster.

Indeed, vampires often feel that they are the victims in any given situation, especially when they are mercilessly feeding upon our energy.

Once we realize that we can gain energy without resorting to vampirism we may be able to curb our desire to feed off the energy of others. In order to effectively deal with the problem of vampirism we need to take two important steps:

- To slay our own vampire and break the vampirism chain
- To become vampire hunters and prevent other vampires from feeding upon us

We can only succeed in self-protection and destruction of vampiric forces when we are prepared to accept both parts of the equation. We all have a potential vampire lurking in the shadows of our subconscious. If we do not recognize this beast it will succeed in winning through and subtly taking control of our lives, squeezing the life out of our relationships and eternally living with us as a detested victim of its own foul hunger. A vampire tastes blood and becomes addicted to it. In the same way an energy vampire becomes addicted to the high of feeding from others, and like many addicts, may not even be able to admit that this predation is taking place. The vampire unknowingly stalks its prey, blissfully unaware that its only desire is the next feed.

As vampires, we must see ourselves clearly for what we are, so that we can finally slay the beast and live in a contented harmony with ourselves and those we love and with whom we live and work.

Fact or Fiction?

Do energy vampires really suck energy from us? Or is this simply a metaphor for a covert communication process? Is it simply a way of explaining, using metaphor, the hidden agenda of many people?

Personally, I am not sure if it matters how you relate to the concept. If you feel there is a real alteration in your energy, then that is true for you. If you prefer to consider it as a metaphorical concept only, it will still work for you.

From my experience and work I have noticed so many distinct changes in energy amongst my clients as well as in myself that I find it difficult to imagine that it is only a psychological concept. I have seen people change, so that their physical features alter from bright and rosy faced to pale and drawn; simultaneously, the energy they had had access to moments earlier seemed to have deserted them leaving them vulnerable, drained and exhausted. All this has been due to different types of vampirism that has caused a drain on the psyche.

We each harbour our own truth within, and my truth will differ from yours. However, if you find your truth in the pages of this book, then my work will be done.

How does Vampire fiction relate to reality?

Vampires are real people, but, unlike the fictional vampire, these do not suck your blood. It is your energy that they crave and that they endeavour to steal. This is the energy that is also your life force and it attracts the undead, which absorb energy from others. The process of absorbing power is a means of making up for a lack of love.

Why Vampires Steal your Energy:

Because it feels unlovable, a Vampire will steal your energy to gain a thrill that will compensate for the lack of love.

Why should a person wish to absorb energy from another?
The process of absorption of energy transfers power to the vampire, and it is this power that the vampire craves.

Inside, the vampire really demands love. It demands to feel loved, and yet simultaneously believes itself to be unlovable.

This creates an untenable conflict; the vampire needs to feel loved so strongly that it is as though its very life depends upon it; that without this demonstration it will fade away and die. The vampire cannot feel alive without love, and, as it is unlovable, can never receive love from another. No matter how much love is offered to the vampire, it will never feel loved. No amount of love will ever be enough to prove it wrong, so fixed is it in this notion. The vampire, however, is a master of manipulation, and creates a curious kind of logic; if it is to be unlovable, it will feed its need for love with power over another.

True Life Tales from the Crypt—Vianex Ltd
In a vampire infested business, Vianex Ltd, the owner decided to solve the problem of moaning, low morale and bullying by putting into place a system of feedback from staff to managers. Instead of alleviating the problem, moaning became worse and worse. The managers at the firm tried to introduce teambuilding activities, these made a momentary improvement, but quickly things went back to the usual moaning and griping, the staff insisting that managers did not understand or care about them.

Eventually the proprietor came to my company to sort the problem out, and from an in depth analysis we were able to clearly identify the problem of vampires. As we explained to the business owner, until these vampires are able to recognise their problem nothing that the business does will be enough. The vampires, individually and on mass, were continually calling for more and more energy, and their insatiability meant that they were simply draining the business and the managers running it.

Demanding or Deserving Love?
A sign of the vampire is its need and demand for love. In other words, it needs love, and it will demand love, but it will not feel that it deserves love. It wants to feel loved, without understanding that love is undemanding. This means that it

cannot gain the feeling it believes it needs, as demanding and love are mutually incompatible.

When we focus primarily on love as a feeling it is possible that the inner vampire is being activated. This causes the energy vampire an inner conflict. In this case, the vampire will settle for a victory of Power rather than Love. It will rather have power over another than risk being open to love and yet potentially not receiving it.

Vampirism occurs when we seek the energy of others rather than finding our source of energy from the universe. In order to find our own energy, without stealing the energy of others, we need to be able to appreciate our self and our connection to the infinite source of energy that exists all around us. The difficulty we often have is in believing that we can do this alone, that we do not need to be "fed". Once we can become self sufficient in our ability to draw energy we stop being vampires.

Love is energy:

The only four-letter word that we are unable to use in business today is love. If you mention the "L" word to business people they are likely to fall off their boardroom chairs. Virtually any other four-letter word will not phase them!

Love is the energy that bonds the universe. It is the essence of life. It cannot be seen, heard or measured, and yet it is the one thing we all live for. Love allows us to reach the souls of others, whatever their culture. Love allows us to empathise, because we all love our children.

Love is all pervading; its strength can alter the course of history and invariably changes our own lives. It is the reason for most things we endure and strive for. It is the reason we work, and yet, in the workplace we do not speak of it.

Frequently we muddle love with sex, and when we talk of one we often imply "the other"! In fact, we may feel freer to speak about sex than we do to talk of love. We may feel that if we were to talk of "love at work" it would be considered subversive as we fear the attention will be upon sexual relationships; something that is rather a distraction to work. If a man were to suggest that "more love" should be brought into the office, it would be met with sniggers as the team would assume he was talking of sex!

In the 1960's and 1970's the Hippies influence was to bring about a middle class acceptance of free sex or "free love" as it was called. The Free Love movement failed because it prohibited people from connecting and therefore was devoid of intimacy. Ang Lee's film "The Ice Storm", set in the 70's demonstrates perfectly how sex without intimacy undoes families and lives.

Love, however, is not just a feeling. It is also a verb. Love as a verb is about giving, about sacrifice for no reward, care and kindness.

By giving, by acting with love as a verb, we can gain more inner energy and strength. In order to give, we need to be able to draw upon our own inner source of love, or draw upon the love that exists in the universe, which you may perceive as beauty, goodness and things that warm your heart. Feelings you can evoke in yourself about yourself. Feeling good about who you are. The greatest form of unconditional love – feeling loved from within, and loved from without.

Fig. 1.1 The Characteristics of a Vampire:	
Mythical Vampires:	**Energy Vampires:**
Come at night when the victim is unaware	Vampires operate by stealth, it is not always obvious when we have been vampirised.
Operate by darkness	Vampires work from the subconscious, and therefore often we are not consciously aware of them. The vampire itself is frequently unaware of its behaviour.
Cast no shadow	Vampires can appear to be perfect, we see only the light and good, and not the dark shadowy parts. Vampires want to maintain this illusion.
Cannot be seen in the mirror	Vampires do not recognize themselves, they do not see how destructive their behaviour is. A vampire detests its own behaviour and shuns this kind of reflection.
Suck the blood of their victims	Energy vampires do not suck blood, but they steal energy.
Encourage mortals to become vampires	They do not recognise another way of life. Some vampires will suggest becoming a vampire. If you asked their advice this would be the option they would choose.
Are insatiably hungry	Energy vampires do not know when enough is enough. They will continue to sap your energy, even when you are exhausted. They have no recognition or empathy, they are totally absorbed in their own world and their own needs.
Often live in nests, with a master vampire.	You may find that where there is one vampire, there are many, each feeding off each other.
Once victims have been "infected" they do not have any option but to continue on that vampiric path.	We become vampires as a result of other vampires feeding from us

How to Recognise a Vampire:

If you imagine the myth as a metaphor for the reality then all the characteristics of an energy vampire can be easily identified.

The Myth in our lives:
As I have already said, the stories of vampires resonate with us because of a truth at the core of them. There is a meaning that is so strong in us we continue to be fascinated by the myth.

As well as the perennial story of Count Dracula, the film of which has been made and remade, updated re-worked, there are some modern vampire stories that provide us with an insight into the way in which the myth works as a metaphor for reality. As the vampire manifests itself in our lives with all the familiar characteristics, we shall begin with their life in the shadows.

Light and darkness—the known and unknown aspects of the self:
An important aspect of the Vampire Theory is the understanding of light and darkness. We are used to these being used to represent good and evil, but in this context we relate to the seen and unseen, what is known and what is unknown about the self; in other words, the conscious and the unconscious mind. The danger of the vampire is that it exists in the shadows of our unconscious.

There it lurks, weaving its cunning entrapments so that we become vampires without realising what has happened to us. The vampire aspect of ourselves is so much cleverer than we *believe* ourselves to be, because the entire resource of the unconscious mind is at its disposal. So vampires operate with unbelievable speed to manipulate and exert power.

When you have been victim to the vampire you may have noticed how it seems to be able to twist and shape situations to create something you find to be unrecognisable as reality.

True Life Tales from the Crypt—Sabrina:
Sabrina decided to leave her abusive husband and take her two children with her. It was an extremely difficult decision to make, but she managed to find a home to rent that was small with a lovely garden and bedrooms for each of them.

Sabrina had to attend Court regarding an injunction against her husband to prevent him from being able to come close enough to her to cause any more injury. It was whilst she was here that he managed to sneak a note to her that read "What have we done, Sabrina? How could we have hurt the children like this? When I see our little ones so sad it makes me realise how we are hurting them. We must try to sort this out. Come back to live with me at home. Come back with the children and lets be a family again."

Sabrina went back. He abused her physically and emotionally, caused her a perforated eardrum and eventually terrorised her until she fled from the family home without the children. Sabrina had been vampirised to the extent that she was unable to see reality as it really was, the vampiric husband was able to bend the truth into an unrecognisable fabrication, and yet she completely bought into it, such can be the power of the vampire.

What are the characteristics of an Energy Vampire?

Energy vampires behave very much like their mythical counterparts, although the myth is a metaphor for the reality. Compare the synopsise and analysis of the three stories/films, Dracula, The Hunger and The Lost Boys.

Dracula, the classic vampire story (see fig. 1.2), encapsulates the myth perfectly. Lucy demonstrates the symptoms of vampirism beautifully. If you have been suffering from vampirism, you may remember waking during the night and being unable to sleep while a situation replayed itself in your head. You may have realised how unsatisfactory that situation was, but at the time, you accepted it unquestioning.

Dracula is afraid of mirrors, he cannot (and perhaps does not want to) see himself. All vampires fail to see themselves in the mirror, It is a sign that the vampire may yet recover when it can begin to make out its face in the vampire mirror, beginning to see that maybe it is we who are the vampires; that they exist within us all.

When Dracula is staked his face becomes peaceful and beautiful again. We therefore can take "heart" that when we are able to allow our heart to open we too can leave the vampires coffin and join the living again.

What does the vampire want from its victims?

In the stories, the vampire appears to need companionship and approval as well as blood. Energy vampires also yearn for approval and companionship. They, too, will encourage others to agree with them and justify their way of behaving. They can be very persuasive in their argument. For example: A vampire may spend time demonstrating how you, as its victim, deserve a better life, and can achieve this by being like it. When you emulate its behaviour you justify it. Vampires will reward you when you behave like them.

In The Hunger, (see fig. 1.3) the vampire's motivation is companionship and love, and yet she uses power and manipulation to achieve these, and pays the price when Victim Sarandon ultimately destroys her.

The Hunger demonstrates that not all relationships in the world of vampires are male/female. In this case a multiplicity are shown, demonstrating the complex web of dissatisfactory relationships that are part of the vampires' lifestyle. The vampire's life appears appealing, and the vampire is herself charismatic and charming, Hence Vampire Deneuve manages to lure Sarandon into a relationship against her better judgement.

Fig 1.2 Fictional Vampires—Dracula by Bram Stoker—Synopsis:

Dracula was originally painted as an ugly character by Bram Stoker, similar to the picture painted in the classic silent film "Nosfaratu". However, when portrayed on screen Dracula is a charismatic and attractive character, very appealing to women. Dracula travels by night, and is afraid of mirrors as his image cannot be seen in them.

The story of Dracula involves a young property agent, Jonathon Harker, who is sent on a mission to Dracula's castle, and who escapes vampirism but unwittingly creates an obsession in Dracula for his wife, Mina.

Dracula comes to England to find Mina and make her his bride. This involves turning her into a vampire. In the process he vampirises her friend, Lucy, who becomes a vampire in turn. Lucy goes through the torment of restless nights and a changed personality, pale and limpid. Eventually she "dies" but becomes one of the "undead" and rises from the grave into an new vampiric existence. Van Helsing, the vampire authority, explains that Lucy's Vampire needs to be destroyed by a stake through the heart

When this is carried out she fights and screams. However, when she is staked her face returns to an innocent beauty, as though the real Lucy is now released and at peace and the Lucy Vampire is destroyed.

When Dracula is finally destroyedhe, too has a look of peace. There was something of the original humanity still in him and it has been released through the death of the vampire.

How do we keep the vampire at bay?

A typical metaphorical analysis of light and dark is that light represents good and dark, evil, but we can also consider that light is what is seen and dark what is unseen. We can interpret this according to ourselves, the light being our self-awareness (that aspect of ourselves that we know) and the dark being the hidden parts of ourselves that lie in the subconscious mind. We can usefully use this to understand and protect ourselves from vampires in day to day life.

First we have to lose the connection between light and good, dark and evil, because this does not serve our purposes, and then begin to consider the other interpretations.

Firstly, the preference of vampires to work in darkness suggests it inhabits the subconscious of the individual, and that it does not like to see its true behaviour in the "light". Therefore, we would probably gain little if we were to tell others when they were allowing their vampire to rise; furthermore, we probably would not realise it if our own had risen from the grave.

Secondly, we know that in the myths journeymen are warned to travel by daylight. So, if we, too, are journeymen, we should remember to keep our awareness activated at all times in order to keep the vampire away.

Fig 1.4 **Fictional Vampires—Synopsis of The Lost Boys(Film):**

A gang of teenage vampires enjoy gorging themselves on their victims, but the leader of the gang is not obvious. It appears to be a young man, played by Keiffer Sutherland in the film. In fact, the real Vampire Master is the book store owner who manipulates the youngsters, letting them believe they are carefree, whilst all the time they are prisoners of their lifestyle and serving his ends.

The two innocent boys who discover this try many different ways of destroying or exposing the Master, especially as he woos their mother. However, when he comes to their house for dinner they find their attempts to use garlic and religious symbols fail.

Afterwards the Master Vampire explains that they could not hurt him as he had been invited into their home, and a vampire is immune if you invite it in. When he explains to their mother how he believes they could be a perfect family, he physically changes and suddenly we can see that he is foul and monstrous, yet at the same time pathetic.

Vampires often appear charismatic or innocent and charming. In the film, The Lost Boys (see fig.1.4), the bookstore proprietor is apparently harmless, wearing spectacles and looking friendly and open faced. He is intelligent, kind and on the surface an ideal mate for the mother. However, he is manipulative and cruel under the surface, out for an unrealistic view of happy family life, where he wields power. Of course, he cannot find happiness with a woman that he has to change before she can become his. This is a recurrent theme with vampires; seeking to change the people they love, doubting their ability to attract love. They choose power over love, as they fear rejection.

Vampires often fail to see beauty in the reality of their lives, but instead continually search for "a better relationship". Their mission is to find the "ideal life/partner/friend". This mission focuses on happiness being found in another person, a different environment or a new job and not on the "inside", in other words, they do not look within, at themselves, to find the truth. Consequently, in their search for perfection, these vampires often leave their partners alone and confused.

How are we vampirised?

There are many different strategies that the vampire will use to deplete you of your hard won energy. We can be drained by the vampire who bullies us, or by the charismatic vampire who woos us, or by the needy vampire who insists on telling us its troubles so that we begin to believe they are our own; or by the vampire who has a wealth of advice for us, or perhaps the one who encourages us to be less than ethical in our treatment of other human beings, claiming that this is only being rational and sensible. Or we may be drained by the vampire who martyrs herself for us, and yet manages to manipulate us into getting what she wants. The strategies vary and although a vampire may have a preferred method, it may not stick to this, if its attempts to vampirise fail, it may swap strategies for another in case that works better.

How are Vampires made?

The story of Dracula makes it clear that to enter a life of vampirism we must first be victims of the deadly bite. Dracula's victims in turn become vampires and walk with the undead, seeking further victims upon whom they can prey. This is true for energy vampires. Once we have been vampirised a vacuum is created within us and that feeling drives us to seek a victim from whom we can quickly and efficiently replenish our lost energy.

Seeking out the energy of another is a quick fix approach, but is ultimately unsatisfactory. As it is not a sustaining source of energy we become quickly depleted and the cycle continues as we again seek a quick energy fix.

Fig 1.3 **Fictional Vampires—Book by Whitley Strieber, synopsis of The Hunger (Film):**
The Vampire, played by Catherine Deneuve, is part of an ancient vampiric race that is fatally flawed in its need to seek humans for companionship and sustenance.
Deneuve and her lover (David Bowie) seek out and feed upon hapless club goers. However, she can only deliver her lovers a lifetime three times longer than usual, and when they begin to age, it happens at an alarming rate.
Bowie seeks out a Doctor (Susan Sarandon) who is a specialist in accelerated ageing and who seeks to find solutions to its effects. He waits twenty minutes for her to see him, during which time his body ages dramatically. When she does meet with him she dismisses him out of hand and he leaves.
Deneuve puts her disintegrating lover in a coffin in the attic, though still (barely) alive, next to her previous lovers. All of which seem to be alive and yet lifeless.
Feeling remorseful about her treatment of the man, Sarandon seeks him out and in the process finds Deneuve is captivated by Sarandon and eventually manages to seduce her.
Once Sarandon has become a vampire even though she resists it, she is compulsively drawn to vampirism.

This process becomes a cascade of vampire upon victim, then victim as vampire upon victim and so on. Whoever is at the bottom of the food chain suffers the most. Often this can be most clearly seen at work, as the individual at the bottom of the chain takes the vacuum home with him or her and commences the vampirism with friends or loved ones.

This process of vampirism can be demonstrated simply. Imagine you have just been vampirised by your boss, you feel drained and upset. Perhaps you feel he has completely stolen your ideas without giving you any credit at all. You leave his office and make straight for the office of your colleague. She is happy to allow you to sit down and vent your feelings. You release all those pent up emotions and then feel energised. Much better. In fact, you really feel quite chipper and decide to take your leave and go back to your work.

Your colleague puts down her pen and decides to take a break. She felt fine before but feels quite exhausted and lacking in motivation now. She decides to go for a walk around the office and find someone to talk to. She does not realise she, too, is becoming one of the walking dead!

This is an obvious form within which the process of vampirism can be seen. However, vampirism can be activated by far subtler, indeed unnoticeable means.

Summary:

An Energy Vampire will seek to drain you of your energy to compensate it for feeling a lack of love in its life.

As a vampire is insatiably hungry no amount of energy will satisfy it.

Understanding the myth helps us to understand Energy Vampires.

Summary of Tips:

To keep your vampire and that of others at bay change your focus. Rather than desiring to feel loved, act out love through the things you do and say. Act lovingly.

Notice the vampiric tendencies in others and then respond by doing something different, and perhaps uncharacteristic. Just changing these patterns can throw the vampire off course.

Vampires are rendered harmless if you do not invite them across your threshold. Switch on the light of your awareness, tell yourself you will not be vampirised, and you will find that the vampire cannot strike.

Chapter 2
Who will the vampire bite?

Discover:
How you know when you have been vampirised.
Why stress and vampires are a dangerous combination.
Why, as victims, we "go back for more".

How you know when you have been a victim of vampirism.

Victims usually become restless during the day and find it difficult to sleep at night. They are drawn to the vampire even though it is harming them.

The effects of vampirism:

Vampirism can occur at any time, and the problem is that it leaves us with that sense of having been drained, feeling listless and tired, dissatisfied, irritated and sometimes even furious. At its worst, it can make us ill.

Usually vampirism takes place during communication, but not always verbally. We can be vampirised by those who use subtle subconscious messages.

When we are having a conversation with a vampire, the first thing we feel is elation. The process of vampirism creates a temporary "high", much like the fictional vampire who finds an erogenous zone when sucking at the neck of its victim; this makes the process enjoyable and even desirable.

After the communication we begin to feel the effects of the energy loss. We notice that we feel dissatisfied, but we often cannot identify exactly what it is that creates this feeling.

Consciously, we believe the incident to be over. It is later that the full affect can be felt; most frequently, in the middle of the night. We awaken in the small hours, one, two or three o'clock in the morning, this sense of "dissatisfaction" has suddenly crystallised and prevents sleep. The mind turns on the events, going over them again and again.

These thoughts may arise at other times, usually when we are relaxing. The vampire manages to sneak into our thoughts when we are not on our guard. Trying to keep it from invading our minds becomes a full time occupation, one that expends even more of our energy.

However, often we choose to allow these thoughts to enter our minds. We enjoy the obsessing, and we loathe it, simultaneously.

As the process of vampirism increases, so the effects increase in intensity. Waking in the night becomes insomnia. Thoughts running around in the head can lead to pacing, an inability to settle, some people wring their hands and rant to themselves. The victim has become trance like. Usual life fades into insignificance as the vampire's needs overwhelm its victim. The victim finds him or herself talking about his or her vampire to others. The vampire can become the centre of the victim's life.

We may think about our vampire excessively, almost obsessively. We can create fantasies around it, so that we believe the vampire to be attractive in some way, either sexually, as a friend, as a mentor, as someone we feel we must care for, or even as someone we must be careful not to offend.

In the day the victim is tired and listless. Focussing on work can be a struggle, thoughts of the vampire can interrupt the day at any point, and the possibility of more vampirism only exacerbates this.

The victim feels drained and tired. He may become irritated and quickly moved to temper, sometimes even fury. This sense of tiredness cannot be improved through rest. The energy loss is intense and does not relate to physical energy. It is an emotional or mental energy that has been sucked and this has to be replaced. When we are giving and receiving love in a non-vampiric relationship we achieve the synergy of energy exchange. This is when both partners become more energised by the exchange than they felt before it.

Fig. 2.1i **Are you vampirised by friends?**

Are your friends really friends, or are you a quick and easy meal ticket? Consider the following and see how many relate to your friends, in each case the possible reason for the energy loss is given below:

She telephones you for a chat and you find you spend the whole time talking about her problems. After the call you worry about her.

Energy Loss: This vampire takes over your life with its troubles. You may find yourself telling your partner or someone else all about it in a bid to relieve you of the feeling the vampire creates. You can feel very loving towards this kind of vampire as it awakens a sense of parental responsibility in you.

He is a good laugh, but it always seems to be at your expense. Still, if you don't take it in good part you will be branded a bad sport.

Energy Loss: The energy loss is felt as the hurt is masked by the apparent joviality you show to your tormentor. This is a form of bullying, and all bullying creates tremendous energy loss.

Fig. 2.1ii **Are you vampirised by friends?**

You resent helping a particular friend, although at the time you willingly offered to do so.

Energy Loss: This smacks of manipulation. You agreed to help because you were subtly manipulated. The after effects include a sense of dissatisfaction and of being used.

She is never on time and always has an excuse. Interestingly when she does arrive she creates a big fuss and is the centre of attention. This is especially likely to happen when it is your big day.

Energy Loss: This vampire feeds off attention and is so jealous of others that it has to outshine everyone. It takes all your energy to remain charming and kind when this vampire apologises too much and remains the focus of attention.

He says he will always be there for you, but you never dare ask him for help because he always has too many troubles of his own. You usually help him out and he usually asks a little bit more of you than you had originally offered.

Energy Loss: This vampire manages to keep you doing its bidding without ever having to return the favour. You find yourself making excuses for him, and not wishing to upset the apple cart by complaining, you say his friendship is valuable. This takes an investment in energy and the dissatisfaction felt under the surface is a huge drain that may not be felt until later. In fact it is the tactic of some vampires to manipulate you into thinking that their life is much more important than yours, and that they are fascinating and exciting people.

You tell your friend a funny story, and she listens with relish and admiration. Then you hear her repeat the story to someone else as though it had happened to her, and not you!

Energy Loss: It is not always apparent how this vampire stole the energy at the time. This one is difficult to detect unless you catch it out. The energy loss can be a slow drip feed affect, whereby the vampire little by little seems to merge with you until you find you cannot distinguish one from the other. This vampire admires you, and that can lead you into a false sense of security. Watch out, it may want to steal your partner as well as your life!

A group of friends go out for a drink and one always manages to be the last to buy the round, either waiting to offer when everyone has a glassful, or coming back with a round of the cheapest beer, and making sure that he times it so that he has to buy the fewest rounds in the evening.

Energy Loss: Its hard work trying to be friendly with someone who seems to cheat your friendship. It is not just the material theft, it is a theft of trust.

You tell her something in confidence and discover that she has told someone else, however, it is difficult to be angry with her as she has such winning ways.

Energy Loss: This vampire uses information like it uses people. It always feels vindicated, and will claim that it has your best interests at heart, and may even convince you that it admires you. The real vampirism occurs when you confront this vampire and find yourself feeling guilty about mentioning the breach of confidence, and you may even find *you* finish up consoling *it*!

Fig. 2.2i **Are you intoxicated by Lovers?**

Is your lover loving you or wielding the power of the vampire over you? If you recognise any of the following you are probably loving the vampire, in each case the possible reason for the energy loss is given below:

Your lover is perfect. You can see no faults in him or her at all.
Energy Loss: You are causing your lover's vampire to rise from the grave. It will find sucking your energy irresistible.

Your lover puts you down, but only by making comments that are almost too trivial to complain about.
Energy Loss: This is typical vampiric behaviour. Being incredibly clever, vampires will not necessarily diminish your self esteem in an obvious way, but instead, to make up for their own sense of inferiority, they will chip away slowly. As you lose self esteem, so the access to your energy potential is also lost and you lose your energy connection to the universe.

Your lover offers to get you a drink in the evening, but at such personal discomfort (aching back etc) that you reassure him/her that you will willingly get it yourself and make sure you get him/her what he/she wants at the same time.
Energy Loss: Using the tactics of martyrdom, this vampire does not state its needs, but instead manipulates. This level of complexity undermines love and creates a gothic and cold environment where vampirism thrives. Very dramatic!

Your lover is incredibly charismatic and attractive, people tell you that you are lucky to be with him/her, but s/he shows little affection to you, saving it all for people s/he hardly knows or who it is "good to be seen with".
Energy Loss: The lack of value your lover ascribes to you reduces your self esteem and therefore becomes de-energising.

Your lover wants to go out with friends, but does not want you to see yours.
Or, your lover always admired your daring dress sense, but now you are together wants you to tone things down.
Energy Loss: Lack of trust due to lack of self love in the vampire. Lack of trust always leads to energy loss.

Your lover jokes about the other women/men s/he has dated, and how they compare to you.
Energy Loss:
Vampires do not feel loveable, and they feel vulnerable about the possibility of losing their partners. One tactic of the vampire is to appear more attractive than it actually feels by covertly criticising its partner. If you have to remain cheerful and accept this behaviour (because if you don't you are being "silly") it causes intense energy loss.

Fig. 2.2ii **Are you intoxicated by Lovers?**

Your lover will not accept that s/he is in a bad mood, and yet manages to upset the whole family, with the blame upon you.

Energy Loss: Blaming behaviours are very draining. This kind of vampirism causes energy loss, often escalates into rows and wastes time when affection could be the alternative. If the vampire recognised its shortcomings and asked for help, rather than blaming it would be less of an energy drain.

You strongly suspect your lover is having an affair, and yet your lover denies it in the face of overwhelming evidence until you begin to doubt yourself and your sanity.

Energy Loss: The energy loss is obvious here, as you fight against impossible odds.

Your lover comes in late from work and, with hand to forehead says "Oh well, I suppose I had better get the dinner".

Energy Loss: This vampire manipulates through guilt. This causes energy loss in its partner as he or she has to deal with it.

Your lover is incapable of helping him/herself, you always have to reassure and look after him/her.

Or, your lover believes you are always being unfair in the way you treat him/her.

Energy Loss: Both of the above are a one way street. All give and no responsibility. You invest energy and the lover takes and feeds from it.

Your lover bullies, rants, is argumentative and cruel.

Energy Loss: Bullying behaviours always cause energy loss as we struggle to raise and maintain an energy shield to protect us, but this drains our energy supply quickly. Your self esteem will fall to an all time low if you remain with a bully vampire. It is not your fault, although this can be difficult to believe, the vampire could choose other ways to behave.

This bears out the Biblical reference to the power that can be accessed "when two or more are gathered together". During this process the transference of love creates the synergy, so that greater love is shed into the universe, perpetuating both communication partners, and a moment of unity is created.

The vampire, however, has always sacrificed love for power. It no longer seeks to give love and enjoy receiving love from others because it does not believe it can gain love without extortion.

A vampire will use a variety of methods to gain your energy, varying from bullying, to crying out for help, to clever and sophisticated methods, such as "teaming up" with you, or appearing attractive and caring, because it does not believe it can gain your love.

Stress and vampires are a dangerous combination.

Pressure of work is generally not that dangerous to us; it usually helps us to rise to the challenge and perform better for short periods. When pressure is combined with vampirism, regardless of whether this is from an individual or the organisation itself, then it can lead to stress and, ultimately, even to "burn out."

The long term effects:

If the process of vampirism goes on unchecked it can lead to "burn out". In other words, that feeling of stress that eventually strips us of ability to function rationally.

Burn out can be described as a complete lack of motivation; permanently physically, mentally and emotionally exhausted. When we are burnt out, we are unable to recuperate with a short break or a rest. Weekends do not re-energise us; the thought of work can reduce us to tears of despair.

Stress is considered to be the cause of burn out. That feeling of being "under pressure" which can initially lift our performance and help us achieve great things, eventually wears us down. We can operate at this "buzz" for short periods. During this "Red Alert" state our bodies prepare for either fight or flight, an archaic response to danger. Now, we rarely need to physically run away from our stressor when it is within working life, instead we need to cope with the deadlines, give that presentation or mete out the punishments or rewards that our organisation demands.

In being under stress at work we have the same physical responses, to fight and flight, our body prepares our limbs for action, by pumping blood to them, our heart rate increases to move oxygen and food quickly to where it will be needed and used. Our breathing may be quicker and shallower. The irises of our eyes dilate to let in more light and allow us to improve our vision. Our gut suffers a loss of blood supply, making it less efficient, as digesting food is not a priority when danger threatens. In extreme cases, our bowels evacuate their contents! Which is why we can get an "upset tummy" when we are nervous. Stress causes more fats to be released into the blood stream ultimately making the clogging of arteries more likely. Stress is a significant factor in undermining our quality of life and our health.

However, pressure can help us to work effectively; many professions rely on this, such as attendants in Accident and Emergency Rooms. It is when workplace pressure is combined with vampirism that burnout will occur and often quickly. It is difficult to function well when we are investing our physical energy into our work, and losing our emotional energy to vampires.

Vampirism as the chief cause of "Burn Out":

A vampiric business will value its people only as a vampire values a human, as a meal ticket. This pernicious attitude takes hold of us and we can come to value ourselves only as the role we carry out. Then we may begin to ask ourselves "Is that all there is to life?". Trying to live up to a role is impossible, we are human beings and not robots. As soon as we try to measure up we identify the areas in which we fail. When we focus on the role we disengage from the person. The organisations that succeed in creating angels will be those that value the individual above the role. These companies will fit the role to the unique human being rather than trying to fit the person to the role.

When our role has more importance than we do, we become insecure and stressed. This is perfect for the vampire who will use any leverage or power at its disposal. Vampires at work are rife, because work gives people power, and vampires rise quickly through the ranks. In my experience "burn out" from highly stressful work is almost always a direct result of vampirism.

This vampirism strips us of our vision, and reduces our self-confidence and self-belief. We lose the passion we felt about the job and find ourselves worrying about the next move we should make and the consequences of our actions only in terms of how the vampire or vampires will manipulate us. We lose sight of the person we are on the inside, we can appear to change personality, to behave irrationally, and yet create (apparently) rational reasons for our behaviour. The most damaging effect of all is the loss of our ability to recognise that we still have potential.

When we feel life is passing us by, or that we have failed it is usually that we have simply been unable to discover our potential. This can make us feel tired and drained from our living our lives. When we rediscover our potential (because it is always there) we can become re-energised and can learn to enjoy our lives again.

People who have "burnt out" at work, often have no understanding of how they can tap into their latent energy once more. As a result, they have often been running on empty for too long, drained by vampirism. Rediscovering your potential is the way to recover from burn out. In order to do this we need to find out how to tap into a source of energy. We consider this in more detail in Part Two - Awakening the Angel.

Fig. 2.3i **Do you work for a Vampiric Organisation?**

Test your organisation's tendency towards vampirism:
If you answer yes to any of the following you may be working for a Vampiric Organisation and/or boss. You need to develop strategies for maintaining your energy and preserving yourself.

Does your company tend to have a high turnover of staff? Does it tend to hire and fire, perhaps making particular job roles redundant and reinventing itself in order to lose certain members of staff?
Yes: Vampiric organisations treat people as expendable resources, if you do not value yourself you cannot value another. Boss vampires are fearfully protective.

Is it considered acceptable for people to shout at each other, or for the boss to shout at their staff when they are not performing?
Yes: Typical of bullying, an obvious, but rarely challenged, form of vampirism.

Does your boss appear to support your ideas, but change his/her mind after the event, or never commit to them?
Or, does he/she have selective memory?
Or, do you feel sapped after a meeting with your boss, even though you did most of the talking and were very enthusiastic at the time?
Or, does your boss tend to tie you up in your own logic?
Yes to any of the above: The vampire drinks in the ideas and then spits out the person. Watch out!

Does the organisation or your working environment have a dense and negative atmosphere?
Yes: Vampires at work. The team may have an unofficial team leader who will lead the group in moaning, just the right amount to create an unpleasant atmosphere. This kind of environment will ultimately result in either low morale and high staff turnover (as the ones who cannot stick will quickly go) and/or a subversive team, who may be sweetness and light with senior managers, and are treated like "pets" by them, but who wield vampiric power over the immediate boss by doing only what is necessary or making decisions about the way in which they should work, with their clan of followers.

Do the people moan about the organisation/boss all the time?
Yes: Loss of energy creates an inertia which is seen when people moan. When moaning the covert message is "I am a victim, I have no power over my life". An organisation that has a healthy can-do culture, and where mistakes are not considered terrible, but instead a part of the learning process, will enable people to lose victim mentality and become proactive.

Fig. 2.3ii **Do you work for a Vampiric Organisation?**

Do people spend a lot of time around the coffee machine?
Yes: Avoidance and victim behaviour. See above.

Do people mistrust the organisation? Is there building of power bases and internal politics?
Yes: Bullying vampires thrive in organisations where politics and power basing can be used to wield power over another. Where there is mistrust, there are vampires; they are either the ones who are not trusted, or the ones who will not trust!

Does the organisation refuse to trust people to make decisions?
Yes: Vampires who want to hold onto power will not give anything away to another, including the ability to make decisions. Making decisions allows us to be in control, and the vampire does not want you to have power, it wants to have it all for itself.

You feel guilty and responsible for your bosses sexual advances?
Yes: Vampires want power. Sexual power is very potent and energising. They do not feed upon the sexual act, they draw energy from the knowledge that they have power.

Why we go back for more.

Being the victim of a vampire feels good. This is only temporary, though, because a process of transformation takes place without our knowledge. As soon as the vampire has stopped feeding we notice our dissatisfaction.

The victim as willing target:

Knowing the vampire has substituted power for love explains why it always seeks to have power over its victims. The storybook vampire has a strange compulsive fascination to the victim. Imagine Lucy from Bram Stoker's "Dracula", seeking the Count at midnight, walking out into the garden in order to offer her neck to him and allowing him to take his fill.

Somehow Dracula managed to create a power over Lucy so that she could not suppress her urgency and need to become his nourishment. Indeed, she clearly felt satisfaction as he fed upon her, as did he.

An energy vampire carefully targets its victim, just as Dracula targeted his. Once the victim has been identified the vampire will home in, and take advantage of the immediate euphoria the process can create for the victim, as well as for the vampire itself.

The Stages of Intoxication:

The illustrations Fig 2.5-7 demonstrate how the victim of vampirism becomes addicted to the process. Just as in the stories, the victim may even seek the vampire out in order to offer his or her neck! The fourth stage, The Transformation, is described in Chapter 4.

The Victim's Intoxication:

Being vampirised feels good. The victim of the vampire often enjoys the experience so much that they put themselves in such a position that they can be fed upon again and again. But, as with Dracula's victim, Lucy, it is after the event that the victim feels bad about him or herself, drained of energy, listless, restless perhaps even suffering from insomnia.

For the victim this experience is intoxicating. It is similar to consuming an addictive drug. The hangover and the remorse come after the event.

Fig. 2.4 **Typical Symptoms of Vampirism:**	
Sleeplessness	Listlessness
Restlessness	Pale.
Uncharacteristic changes in behaviour.	Tired in the day.
Waking up in the morning feeling as tired as at bed time.	Fearful—of nothing specifically.
Feeling stressed.	Snapping at loved ones.
Tired in the day.	Suddenly losing patience with people.
Need to revert to drugs and alcohol to "relax" after work.	Feeling joyless and that life is passing you by.
Pointlessly replaying an event in the mind, or discussing it repeatedly to no gain or end result.	Wanting to spend all day talking, without doing—especially at work.

Fig. 2.5 **The Stages of Intoxication:** **Stage 1—The Snare**		
Stages	**What is happening**	**How you are feeling**
1. The Attraction 	The vampire sees you as a potential source of energy. You become attractive to the vampire.	You may not be aware of this. You may notice the vampire and feel drawn. A vampire can often create a subconscious longing for it in its victims.
2. The Approach 	The vampire makes a effort to seek you out and then approaches you. When the vampire makes its initial approach it is testing your susceptibility to vampirism. If you are open it will proceed with the bite.	You have no reason to suspect its motives, your guard is down. You may even feel pleased and honoured to have been sought out.
3. The Bite 	The vampire engages you with the bite. At this point it has you "trapped".	You may have been in a rush to leave, but suddenly you find you have all the time in the world for the vampire. Something keeps you. It is a pleasant feeling.

Fig. 2.6 The Stages of Intoxication: Stage 2— The Energy Drain

Stages	What is happening	How you are feeling
4. The Sucking	Once the vampire has bitten it will begin to suck your energy.	You are drawn in. Perhaps the vampire compels you to advise it, but it tells you that everything you suggest will fail for it. Perhaps it becomes more rather than less needy, perhaps you just can't stop talking—but don't know why! At this moment you may feel euphoric.
5. The Withdrawal	When it realises the feed has come to an end it will withdraw, leaving the two puncture marks in the neck that we recognise as being the mark of the vampire.	You feel sad or disappointed when the moment comes to an end. The euphoria is over without a conclusion. Punctures in the neck enable subsequent energy leakage to occur easily.
6. The Vacuum	The energy has been sucked from the victim and leaves a vacuum, an empty space within.	A feeling of dissatisfaction sets in. It is now that you feel uncomfortable, unhappy or tormented by the experience. Often with no way of rationalising why. It may feel like a "hangover".

Fig. 2.7 **The Stages of Intoxication: Stage 3—The Addiction**		
Stages	**What is happening**	**How you are feeling**
7. The Return	If this "feed" proved satisfactory, the vampire will return for a further feed.	Once back in contact with the vampire, the victim may wish to recreate that euphoric feeling of having the energy drained from him/her.
8. The Intoxication	After this cycle repeats the victim may quickly become intoxicated and seek out the vampire in order to provide its next "meal".	Without understanding why, the victim desires to be with the vampire more than anything. Even if brutalised by the vampire, the victim will still want to go back for more, believing the vampire loves him/her and that he/she loves it.

Summary:
Having energy sapped can feel quite pleasant at the time. It is only afterwards that you feel exhausted, listless and dissatisfied. You are likely to have a sleepless night in the worst cases.
The long term effect of pressure combined with vampirism is burn out, which is when you lose the energy and ability to do anything for yourself. This can happen in work or within a personal relationship.

Summary of Tips:
Notice when you feel the symptoms of vampirism and identify what happened to cause them. Knowing why you feel as you do helps to reduce the negative effects, and will help you to sleep better.
Avoid stress by creating a balance in your life. Cut out caffeine (a couple of coffees can double the level of adrenalin in the system) and take time out to relax.
When you notice you are becoming drawn into a vampiric exchange, withdraw from the situation in order to give yourself time to rethink—even a quick trip to the bathroom can be enough to alter the energy flows in the communication.

The Charismatic Vampire

Chapter 3
Recognising the Different Energy Vampires

Discover:
Whether you are likely to become a victim of vampirism.
Which of the six different vampires prey upon you.
Whether you are an Energy Vampire

Are you likely to become a victim of Vampirism?

Vampires may exist in our homes, places of work, amongst our friends and lovers. You are as likely to be a victim of vampirism regardless of whether you see yourself as strong and self confident or vulnerable and diffident.

Natural Prey:
Many people find themselves natural prey for vampires. Sometimes these people are the vulnerable, perhaps with lower self-esteem; sometimes they are those with great passions and seemingly inexhaustible energy.

Frequently, the most insidious of the vampires will target a victim just because he or she is positive, able, and perhaps has a cogent personality. People who are self-sufficient, self-approving and self-accepting are good victims. In other words, a vampire's prey is as likely to be a strong person as a vulnerable one.

Being able to find your own source of energy does not make you immune from vampires. In fact, it makes you more desirable as a source of nourishment.

People with whom we have an on-going relationship carry out the most effective vampirism upon us. Energy can be described as the universal power of love, but this does not mean that it applies only to romantic love. However, vampirism is frequently rife in our relationships with our lovers.

Controlling and Manipulative Vampires:
We see vampiristic relationships in work, at home, with loved ones, friends, in fact anywhere that we have a relationship with another human there may be vampirism occuring. Vampires can work by either controlling or manipulating. In other words, they may seek us out and prey upon us (controlling) or lure us into feeding them (manipulating). However, do not be fooled into thinking that

a controlling vampire is more dangerous than the manipulative. They are both monstrously hungry and hell bent on getting what they want—your energy.

Strong and Vulnerable Victims:
Victims may also be either vulnerable or strong. It may be a surprise to realise that vampires will often seek out the strong upon whom to feed. The Manipulative Vampire may find a satisfying meal in the energy of a strong and, on the face of it, self sufficient, competent and capable person. Gender is not important, as active or passive victims and vampires can actually be of either gender. Sexual orientation is also irrelevant in terms of vampirism. Lovers of either sex or orientation may fall prey to, or themselves become, vampires.

Manipulative Vampires:
Manipulative Vampires do not exert an obvious control, they do so by covert means. They sap your energy by manipulation. These Manipulative Vampires may appear to be weak when they are exerting the most control, and this is the problem for the victim. Victims can be both weak themselves, or may be strong, in either case, they fall into the trap of vampirism without realising, and when the vampire has sunk its teeth in, it is difficult to break away, the victim is infected and the deadly attraction to the vampire has begun.

Controlling Vampires:
The active type may blast you with charisma, or bully. You are aware of their influence, even if you are not aware of their ability to use this to control. Controlling Vampires will seize upon your passion, and either suck it dry and use your ideas against you, or squash it, undermine it until you feel confused about your real motivation, and begin to buy into theirs. Vampires are always hungry, they do not know the meaning of enough. This vampire will weave its spell so that you are hooked on the thrill of its presence, or disempowered and at the mercy of its might.

Some vampires can drain you just by their presence. This is typical of the bully vampire. These are not always recognised as bullies at work, they maybe seen as "hard nosed" and driven by a "sole interest in the bottom line".

Beware of your own Vampire:
When considering each of the vampires types it is most important to see whether we can recognise these qualities in ourselves. Remember, we all have the potential for vampirism within us, and seeing only the vampires in others is an example of allowing our own to rise from the grave.

Which of the six different vampires prey upon you?

The six different vampires are likely to strike at different times and places, but we need to be vigilant and guard against them all.

- The Corrupter Vampire—seeks to corrupt you
- The Intimidating Vampire—a bully
- The Needy Vampire—seeks your help
- The Charismatic Vampire—blinds you with charm
- The Guilt or Maternal Vampire—creates feelings of guilt
- The Advisor or Paternal Vampire—acts as your mentor

In her excellent book "Unholy Hungers" Barbara Hort defines a number of Vampire Types within intimate relationships.

Type 1 Corrupter Vampire:
Controlling Vampire, Strong Victim

> Corrupter Vampires will lure you into a life of vampirism, using and abusing anyone who gets in their way. They tread on toes, bully, lie and cheat their way up the ladder. They may come to a sticky end on the way back down!

These are vampires who achieve their ends by disguising their inner base natures. They often appear successful and enviable, but have a secret side to their lives. They may weave a web of fiction around themselves, creating lies about who they are, where they come from, and anything else. The lies can become confused with reality, and they are often very poorly equipped to deal with direct questions to their integrity.

The Corrupter is often amazingly youthful in appearance, as though it has "sold its soul to the devil". However, there is usually a pay back time, but the victims can be destroyed by the Corrupter before this comes home to roost.

How do the victims of Corrupter Vampires react?
Often the victims will envy and aim to follow the lead of this vampire, believing in the self created and perpetuated myth. Victims may fail to accept that the Corrupter has a darker side. Victims become corrupted; they lose their identity and are absorbed into the life of the Corrupter, so that the distinctions between Vampire and Victim are thin and indistinguishable.

The characteristics of an organization within which vampires thrive:
Companies in which vampires thrive (and perhaps have power) tend to have hire and fire policies, internal politics, power building and negative communication. People can feel exhausted by their usual day to day life, stress is rife and even the vampires are dissatisfied by their lives.

True Life Tales from the Crypt:
Robert Maxwell and some other disgraced political figures are good examples! In addition, the Kray Brothers, the 1960's London gangsters, would be good examples of this corrupting vampire.

This kind of vampire is so intent on maintaining its position, and yet has so many opportunities to see its own faults, it becomes obsessive in its attempts to appear perfect.

This drive for creating an illusion of perfection can even cause it to bankrupt itself with expensive court cases or litigation to deny rumours or accusations in the media about its motives or behaviour. Or, in the case of some criminal vampires, it can even kill. In a commercial situation this means it may be fiercely "political", love to utilise rumour and gossip, and will usually get its way, but without stating its needs.

The Corrupter may raise its ugly head in loving relationships where the Vampire wishes to corrupt its victim, such as trying to draw the victim into sexually "open relationships", "swinger" parties etc. In this way, the vampire wields the power over its victim, playing on her vulnerabilities and, at the same time, demonstrating the power it has over her.

Vampires who want to have this kind of sexual experience do so out of self-hatred, and therefore do not believe in their ability to have an intimate relationship. Intimacy demands exposing one's inner truth, and anonymous sex is a means of feeling attractive without having to be intimate and reveal what one believes to be an unattractive truth about oneself.

Corrupter Vampires like to be surrounded by people who will agree with them, and they may constantly rationalise their decisions. Even when those decisions are obviously outlandish and beyond reason, it is difficult to argue against them. Once you have asserted yourself with a Corrupter Vampire you are unlikely ever to receive its confidence and protection again.

Fictional Case Study—Wall Street – Film
An example is Gordon Gecko (played by Michael Douglas) in the film "Wall Street". He plays a highly successful investor who, as he is a fascinating figure, manages to cajole a young stock broker (played by Charlie Sheen) into

committing an offence that will make them both a lot of money. Gecko does this by selling the young stockbroker a vision of life with wealth, and encourages him to believe he can emulate Gecko's own life, totally.

Wall Street demonstrates the paternal vampire well, in particular showing how Sheen loses sight of his own personality (a symptom of vampirism) as represented by his separation from his own father (a manual worker and union man, played by Martin Sheen) and his apparent "adoption" by Gecko.

Fictional Case Study– Interview with The Vampire:

In the book "Interview with The Vampire" by Anne Rice, and the subsequent film, Louis De Pointe, a vampire, tells a journalist his strange life that has stretched two centuries.

He explains how he was lured into a life of vampirism by another, the vampire, Lestat. The vampire explains how the appeal of the life of the vampire was made so apparent to him that he became transfixed by both his mentor and his lifestyle, yet he found it difficult to prey on humans. After a while his hunger got the better of him, as he was continually in the company of the draining mentor and desperately needed to feed.

The only thing that would satisfy his hunger was the blood of a human. So he fell into the depravity of vampirism, a life with no way out. The two male vampires adopted a young female orphan and finally the push and pull of loyalty and ethics in this weird undead family created lethal results.

The homoerotic themes in this story highlight the concept of vampirism as a sacrifice of love for power. In this instance the power exerted is suggestively sexual. However, that aside, the themes are compatible with Energy Vampires as a metaphor.

Lestat is lonely and tries to seduce or bully companions. He does not trust his ability to be loveable, so he wields power and sells this life of vampirism as perfect, as the gains are immense. In fact they are material, and the lack of love could almost kill the vampire if he were not immortal. Immortality becomes a curse and not a blessing when one's life is lacking in real and wholesome love. Vampires fear garlic for the same reason, as it represents wholesome, healing and simple nourishment, a metaphor for simple love.

By adopting a child the vampires seek to seal their union and yet the child is like a cuckoo in the nest, and can outstrip even Lestat's hunger. This can frequently be seen in organisations, where the vampire boss encourages the subordinate to behave as it does in order to wield power in the business. The subordinate, once he has learnt how to vampirise, may quickly usurp his mentor. There is no loyalty in vampirism.

Type 2—The Intimidating Vampire:
Controlling Vampire, Vulnerable Victim

> Intimidating Vampires will bully believing that only they are right, and that to get what they want they have to use force or fear.

They may think that they are being assertive, but Intimidating Vampires are using aggressive bullying tactics to get you to do what they want. You find yourself trapped by your own logic, and agreeing with them. They never proclaim it to be necessary to be reasonable, because they have "right" on their side. Intimidating, bully vampires loathe the joy of others and seek to have it, or destroy it.

How do the victims of these vampires react?
You use a lot of energy trying to fend them off, and may feel exhausted just being near them. You could liken it to Star Trek, where the Starship Enterprise has its energy shields raised on full power! After a while the engine is drained, something has to give, and when the shields go down the "ship" is vulnerable again. Raising protective energy shields is an ineffective device as it depletes our energy and therefore disconnects us from our energy potential.

How do you know if you have been a victim of an Intimidating Vampire?
Some vampires can drain you just by their presence. This is typical of the bully vampire. These are not always recognised as bullies, they may consider themselves "practical" or "down to earth". However, whether they appear in working or domestic life a bully vampire will leave you feeling exhausted and tender. Your self confidence dented.

True Life Tales from the Crypt—Phyllis:
Phyllis, was the ruthless and hardnosed manager of the Finance department. She used fear and politics to lever weaker victims to achieve her desires. Shouting and always thrusting a piece of paper under the noses of her victims, she would demonstrate that the figures were never good enough. She would use "black and white arguments" there was no middle ground. Her most detested victims were the sales people. They were easy targets, and by haranguing them she managed to keep them under such immense pressure they would be bound either to make promises they could not keep or mistakes that she could criticise and use as examples for others. Her reign of terror reduced men and women alike, to tears. Phyllis would keep

a few close allies (victims), however she was not nice to them. Her closest ally (victim) would feel pressured to follow Phyllis's line, even though she would feel it was not right, crying out "I have to run with the fox and hunt with the hounds".

Type 3—The Needy Vampire:
Manipulative Vampire, Strong Victim

> Needy Vampires seek "rescuers". They drain you with their problems until you feel responsible for them.

Needy Vampires need your help, and you want to nurture and help them. They are very grateful to the help you give on the surface, telling you how much they value you and everything you know and do.

They will usually complain to other people about you, and say things like "I thought you were my friend" if you want them to stand on their own two feet.

They make you feel powerful, but when you have finished with them you are exhausted and often dwell on their problems more than your own!

The Needy Vampire will cry out "its not fair" time and again. "I have awful luck", "Life never treats me right". They do not believe they are in control of their own destiny and so seek out people from whom they can gain the power to change their lives. Unfortunately, the Needy Vampire will always be disappointed by their Victim in the end, because there is no elusive power "out there" it is within the individual him or herself.

The Needy Vampire may well call you its best friend one minute and worst enemy the next. Needy Vampires will then tell other people (new prey) how badly you treated them. This can be a shock to the innocent prey, who thought that by "helping" whether practically or through emotional support, he or she would be appreciated and cherished.

This type of vampire will seek out the strong because weak people will provide an inadequate meal. Needy Vampires often arrive as friends, and we can be mistaken for thinking they are very true and loyal to us. In fact, they are only interested in a quick fix. Be especially wary of Needy Vampires who want to become your lover. They will appear exciting and yet sad and affecting, which can be compulsive. The vampire's prey believes it can have a loving affair, whilst giving extra comfort to the vampire. The Needy Vampire will always be weakened and incapable of taking action, it will make its prey feel strong and able, and so the sense of responsibility of prey over vampire is reinforced. The Needy Vampire excuses itself by claiming that it could never have the ability, strength of character, etc of its prey. The danger here is that the vampire's prey is being drawn into a relationship in which he or she will be drained and used, even though the vampire itself feels it is abused in the relationship.

How do the victims of Needy Vampires react?

Initially the victim feels good. She or he is helping, being compassionate and receiving appreciation from the vampire for this. This confers a sense of satisfaction at the time. However, almost immediately afterwards the victim feels exhausted. The problems of the vampire become his or her own. Victims can begin to obsess about them, and eventually feel as though the distinction between the vampire's problems and his or her own life has become blurred.

Fictional Case Study—My Blue Eyed Boy—Novel by Helen Dunmore

This book is rife with needy vampires. Simone, is working hard at a responsible job as a District Judge in order to help support her husband, Donald, who is on the verge of bankruptcy. Donald's unrealistic attempts to make money leave him falling further and further into despair, relying more upon Simone. She has to support him emotionally, and so is effectively rescuing him from his feelings of inadequacy. She finds this draining.

To support the view that we tend to attract vampires, consider Simone, who receives a letter from an old boyfriend of 20 years ago, another Needy Vampire, who has been emotionally troubled and through treatment and yet is now back in her life, creating yet another wounded puppy for her to deal with. This one is obsessive and could upset her whole life.

True Life Tales from the Crypt—Sue and Angie:

Sue offered to foster her best friend and lodger Angie's baby as she was going through a bad time with her partner and was unsure of whether she wanted to keep the baby or not. Angie gladly accepted the offer from Sue, and she had little to do with the baby's upbringing as she was frequently too tired.

Angie needed constant reassurance and care from Sue, who felt she had two babies to cope with, but as time went by she was impressed with how Angie improved. Angie eventually got a CV together and applied for some jobs, securing a part-time customer service position. However, after six months Sue had to ask Angie if she could find a new room because she was expecting a baby herself. Angie said she understood, and Sue helped by providing information on a few possible lodgings that would be suitable and affordable. Angie left, deciding that she could now cope with looking after her baby, however, she refused to ever speak to Sue again. She told their mutual friends that Sue had been mean, and that she should have given her more notice. She complained that she had helped Sue out with rent for several years and that Sue obviously cares nothing for her, but, as Angie told everyone who would listen, "that's the sort of person that always seems to take advantage of me."

True Life Tales from the Crypt—Alison and Jo:

Alison wanted to do something about the relationship she had with Jo. Her reason for seeking one -to-one coaching was because she felt she could help Jo out of her troubled marriage. Jo's husband was violent and constantly critical.   As a result Jo's self esteem was poor and she doubted her ability in even the simplest task. After a short time Alison realised that it was not Jo that she should be helping but herself. She discovered that Jo's neediness was affecting her own life and health. Alison had already taken Jo in and "protected" her from a violent outburst from her husband. She was helping to prepare Jo to leave him, as she was worried for Jo's safety. However, whatever suggestion Alison made was greeted with "Yes... but" from Jo, who was never prepared to commit to any of the very sound ideas. Alison's energy was being used to prop up Jo who had become a Needy Vampire as a result of the abuse from her husband.

Type 4– Charismatic Vampire:
Controlling Vampire, Vulnerable Victim

Charismatic Vampires are captivating. You may seek them out, but feel strangely drained and dissatisfied afterwards. They will feed on your ideas and your passion, and drop you when you no longer provide an adequate meal.

Charismatic Vampires command attention. If they give you attention you feel entranced and find yourself telling them everything. They will listen to every word, making deep eye contact.

When you have finished you feel dissatisfied, vulnerable, you may feel that you have said too much. You often forget this the next time you see them. Later, you may catch them repeating what you have said to someone else as if it was their idea!

Fictional and Mythical Charismatic Vampires:
The story of Dracula has already been described in Chapter 1, but he is the archetypal Charismatic Vampire. Although Dracula's original incarnations

were foul and ugly, the Charismatic Vampire has the outward appearance of the dashing and attractive figure we so frequently associate with vampires. Dracula is often the subject of sexual fantasy, for either vampire or victim, and

Fig 3.1 **Who has Vampirised you?** **Quick Quiz:** If you answer yes to any of the following, then you have probably been the victim of a vampire. In which case read on and discover what type of vampire may have been responsible:	
	Yes
1. Have you ever felt wasted by someone, or by certain relationships? *If yes, then you could have been vampirised by any of the different vampire types.*	
2. Do you seem to attract energy sapping people? *If yes, perhaps you are a magnet to vampires, especially the Needy type.*	
3. Does your partner/friend imply but not declare clearly what s/he needs or wants from you? *If yes, perhaps s/he is a Guilt Vampire.*	
4. Do you find your friends to be more draining than supportive? *If yes, they may be Needy Vampires if they are always asking you to share their problems.*	
5. Do you ever feel people manipulate you with feelings of guilt? *If yes, this is often the Guilt Vampire*	
6. Do you agree to helping people and later feel "put upon?" *If yes, it is most likely a Needy Vampire has woven its spell on you.*	
7. Do people seem to take advantage of you all the time? *If yes, it could be that they are Intimidating Vampires, Advisor or Corrupter Vampires*	
8. Do you have a friend/partner who is extremely attractive and charismatic and yet you frequently feel unvalued by him/her? *If yes, it is likely to be the Charismatic Vampire*	
9. Do you find yourself doing things of which you do not approve because a friend/ partner has managed to convince you to? *If yes, it is probably a Corrupter Vampire.*	
10. Do your friends seem to have huge amounts of advice to offer you, making it difficult to drag yourself away, and leaving you trying to find excuses for not carrying out what they are convinced is right for you? *If yes, they are probably Advisor Vampires.*	

the close association with sexuality is not accidental. The charisma of the vampire is often (but not solely) associated with sexual attraction (or can be confused with it). This is not always overt, and cannot be assumed to be heterosexual. The stories of vampires are as frequently same sex attraction, such as the two women in The Hunger by Whitley Strieber, or the two male characters (and perhaps the journalist too) in Interview with The Vampire by Anne Rice.

The sexual attraction of the charismatic vampire can be used within non sexual relationships, and may also overlap with the Paternal Vampire, who mentors us. This can most often be seen within working relationships.

How do you know if you have been a victim of a Charismatic vampire?

You may have had an experience when you met someone very attractive, who commanded attention when he or she entered the room, and who seemed really interested in you. It wanted to know everything about you and continually asked questions. You may have found yourself answering, even though you were sometimes surprised at you own frankness. Yet *you* seemed to captivate *it*. However, later you may have felt uncomfortable, but unable to pinpoint why. When you reflected on the meeting it seemed there was something wrong. You enjoyed it at the time, and yet after felt bad, even abused. Strangely, you will probably find that if this vampire comes back into your life you will go through the same thing all over again.

True Life Tales from the Crypt—George:

George was a charismatic vampire who created an atmosphere within his business in which all the staff became intoxicated. They would all need to tell him their ideas, and he would let them talk and talk. Fiona, the sales manager, would give him her energy and ideas, and he would appear to drink them in, making her feel more enthusiastic and increasing her commitment. It was only later that she felt drained, without understanding why. Fiona introduced George to a new method of monitoring sales people, but found that George would use her own ideas against her, when it suited him, without any remorse at all. Eventually George told Fiona that her system of monitoring activity would be used to identify her management failings. Fiona's approach was usually motivational, but she felt forced to use unnatural and ultimately destructive management methods, losing some loyal staff, but increasing (notionally) the profitability of the business. Fiona did manage to catch George out, but it was she who had to leave the company, burnt out and de-motivated. Many charismatic vampires are never caught out.

Type 5—Guilt or Maternal Vampire:
Manipulative Vampire, Vulnerable Victim

> Guilt Vampires will make you feel guilty in order to manipulate you into remaining "there for them". They are good at disempowering others.

Maternal vampires may be male or female, but this vampire smacks of the Mother–Daughter guilt ridden relationship that can fester where jealousy, lack of trust and low self esteem in the mother and daughter are rife.

This vampire wants you to carry a torch for it, it wants to be a mentor and yet is jealous of your success, and will find any opportunity to undermine your ability while appearing devoted. "I'm sorry you failed, keep trying" it will say, with apparent supportiveness.

The guilt vampire will sap your energy by making you rescue it. It will live its life through the success of others, whilst blaming them for its failure, or, more accurately, cleverly making them feel guilty for "holding it back". The guilt vampire will maintain victims by, itself claiming to be a victim, drawing the strength from others as its only source of sustenance.

It can be an intensely "push and pull" type of relationship, whereby the vampire appears to wish you well and urge you on, but will stop short of the final push, by using guilt to draw you back again. Furthermore, it will even undermine you and, if it is your boss at work, this vampire will drop hints at meetings where you are not invited, voicing its doubts about *your* ability! It is subtle and cunning, and manages to appear to have everyone's, but its own, best interests at heart, whereas in fact the reverse is true.

Fictional Case Study—Working Girl - Film
An ideal example of the guilt vampire is Sigourney Weaver's character, Katherine, in Working Girl. She appeared to be encouraging her young protégé, Tess (Melanie Griffith). But actually Katherine only wanted the glory for herself. Tess is Katherine's secretary, she has all the relevant qualifications to move into a position in investment, but can't seem to get a break.

Tess is taken in by the superficial care she is given by her boss, and believes that she will really help her to succeed, and so she tells her of an idea that could be very profitable. Her boss promises to look into it, but returns with the disappointing news that it will not be acceptable. She urges Tess to keep trying, and implies she will be supporting her all the way.

Tess believes her boss is being particularly caring and helpful because she is a woman, and feels they have a kind of solidarity. It is only by chance that she finds out her idea was not turned down out of hand, as her boss had told her, but that her boss was going to steal the idea for herself.

Tess is duped by Katherine who claims they are "practically sisters", and yet who has no compunction about using her and preventing her rise within the firm. All the while Tess defends Katherine as she sees her as someone who will nurture and care for her, helping her achieve the big break for which she is searching.

How do the victims of Guilt/Maternal Vampires react?

The victim will love the attention, but is stifled by the limitations that she feels are imposed upon her (usually by beliefs the vampire has subtly implanted that its victim lacks the necessary ability). The victim will often feel she is incapable of escape. She may remain working for the vampire for years. It is the vampire that really is incapable of escape, and therefore it is cruelly critical of anyone who does move on, undermining with fabricated evidence that he or she will never gain another job, home or lifestyle of a similar calibre. In any case, the vampire and the victim are unable to shift the relationship from a basis of guilt to one of two adults, neither needing to steal energy.

True Life Tales from the Crypt—Darren:

The covertly ambitious manager, Darren used this technique to sap the energy of the person he considered to have the real talent, his assistant, Helen. Helen felt a sense of responsibility to the weaker and ineffectual Darren. He constantly whined about how much better she was than he, and how he needed her to help him. Whilst promising her the trappings of success and occasionally demonstrating that they were making progress, he maintained her commitment and sympathy. However, most of the time he kept her insecure by revealing how "their" work was not appreciated by the company, but convincing her that they needed to persevere.

Eventually Helen's resolve was so weakened that she was vulnerable to Darren's sexual harassment. She gave in to sex, feeling guilty and responsible for leading him on; in her view, Darren was the weak one.

Darren knew that Helen was very loyal and used this loyalty to ensure she remained within his power. Quickly, Helen began to realise how she was being abused and started to deny Darren's advances. As a result Darren had Helen sacked as the relationship was becoming dangerous, although he demonstrated both grief and disappointment when she left, and claimed he was unaware that this was going to happen, in fact he had orchestrated it as a part of his rise to further power and self protection.

Type 6—Advisor or Paternal Vampire:
Controlling Vampire, Strong Victim

> Advisor Vampires are mentors who will lure you into a life of vampirism.

Advisor or Paternal Vampires appear to be perfect, almost an ideal role model. This vampire wants to be your advisor, and is very powerful in this role. It appears to know what is best, and appears to have your best interests at heart (actually it is unable to see beyond its own best interests and feelings). It may change direction, and insist you follow its advice, or otherwise will happily "leave you to rot".

Advisor Vampires feel a thrill from offering their advice. They can talk and talk, and will often talk over you when you try to mention your own situation, because, after all, they claim they are doing this "for *your* benefit".

The Advisor finds it difficult to believe that it is not being helpful, but in fact the energy is moving from the victim or "mentored" to the vampire. The Advisor will feel greatly energised by being able to share its profound "wisdom", whilst failing to realise that real wisdom is in knowing how to stop, and when enough is enough.

The Advisor feels that it has so much to offer its victim, that everything is a gem and nothing can be omitted. The Advisor is likely to tell others how important it was to the victim, glorifying in its ability to help and guide.

How do the victims of Advisor/Paternal Vampires react?
You can become disempowered by the need to gain approval and lose confidence in your own decisions as you feel you have to "check in" with the advisor, "just in case ...." This kind of vampire is typical of those who "do not cast a shadow" – that is, it appears perfect, and by viewing it as perfect you will help the vampire to rise.

Fictional Case Study—Tootsie - Film
Dustin Hoffman plays the "know it all" actor who cannot get a job because he is too difficult to work with. To prove his worth he takes on the role of a woman in a television soap opera, his true sex being unknown to the director and cast. Hoffman falls in love with an actress (played by Jessica Lange) on the cast, who takes to him because he is able to offer her help and advice with her lines. Hoffman discovers that when he is himself (and male) he is domineering and uncaring with his friends and lovers, that he is so full of his own self-importance and knowledge that he fails to realise that this is creating people

who are dependent upon him, in particular, his girl friend Sandy, who becomes his lover and then is completely forgotten by him, so that he fails to keep any dates with her.

Eventually he has to come clean, and reveals to Lange, the women he loves, that "I was a better man as a woman than I ever was as a man".

Hoffman's character was able to realise the difference between "telling" and being the centre of attention, and "sharing" and being part of a joint experience. He was able to slay his vampire!

Fig 3.2 **Are you an Energy Vampire?** **Quick Quiz:**	
If you answer yes to any of the following, then you have probably used vampirism in which case notice the vampire type and refer back to it in the chapter.	
This time notice how these vampiric traits may be demonstrated by *you*.	If Yes:
1. Do you ever feel you are sapping the energy of others?	*You must be a vampire! But which one?*
2. Do you feel you are trying to get a response from someone, perhaps through manipulating them to support you?	*You are probably using a Guilt or Needy Vampire strategy*
3. Do you need to be the centre of attention, have people hang on your every word or admire you?	*You are being a Charismatic Vampire as they love to hold "court".*
4. You sometimes get what you want by dropping big hints or making people feel guilty?	*Guilt as a weapon signifies the Guilt Vampire.*
5. Do you have friends upon whom you rely to be supportive and give you a boost when you need it?	*Its your Needy Vampire who loves to be rescued and to have friends "cheer it up".*
6. Do you ever moan about other people? Do you feel life is particularly bad for you?	*This is your Needy Vampire, "everything is unfair and there is nothing I can do about it" is its cry.*
7. Do you ever "cheat the system" and encourage others to join in the scam?	*This is the Corrupter Vampire in you who likes to share a lack of morality*
8. Do you have to threaten people in order to make them pull their weight?	*You may be an Intimidating Vampire. These always seems to be surrounded by people who are incompetent! This vampire is too busy being "right" to appreciate the unique gifts of others.*
9. Do you find that you have a way of inspiring people to do things that *you* believe are in their best interests, even when you do not know the whole situation?	*You may be the Advisor Vampire who likes to be a mentor, but it is clearly vampirism if you are only interested in your self importance as a mentor.*

Are you an Energy Vampire?

We all hold the potential to be a vampire, and yet we often find it far easier to recognise this trait in others than we do in ourselves.

When we notice a vampire, it means we are vampires! That is quite a daunting prospect and one that may make you want to throw this book away! But the truth is that we must look within to see how we may be unwittingly falling into the vampire's lifestyle.

We know that once a vampire has preyed upon us, we begin a transformation into the beast. So for every one of us who has been victimised by a vampire we must expect to be demonstrating those same vampire traits.

The more we deny this the less chance we have of making real changes in our lives that will rid us of vampires forever.

We may be able to recognise the vampire in others very easily, but when we see it within ourselves we know we have come home to a truth that will enable us to elevate our relationships to an angelic status. We can be angels and live amongst angels. Honestly consider the questionnaire to see if this sheds any light on the techniques you use to get what you want in life.

Summary of Tips:

Avoid counter attacks. You never need to give this vampire reasons, If you say no, mean no and move on.

Do not get drawn into the drama. Take everything they say at face value but know that the vampire is trying to manipulate.

Fig 3.3 Summary of Vampire Types and their Victims		
	Controlling Vampires	*Manipulative Vampires*
Strong Victims	**Advisor** or **Paternal** takes control by relentlessly giving advice even if it does not know the whole story.	**Needy** manipulates by being weak and relying on you to rescue it.
	Corrupter will draw you into dubious activities, in order to "beat the system" so that you become as "thick as thieves".	
Vulnerable Victims	**Charismatic** controls you by luring you in through its attractiveness, making you feel important .	**Guilt** or **Maternal** manipulates by playing the martyr and preying on your guilt.
	Intimidating controls through aggressive and bullying tactics.	

Chapter 4
The Vampire Within

Discover:
How a victim becomes a vampire.
How to lose the vampire lifestyle.
How to keep the vampire at bay.

How a victim becomes a vampire

All vampires are made by vampires. When the Vampire drains its victim of energy, the victim will be prone to replace the lost energy by unwittingly transforming into a vampire. And so the cycle continues.

Vampires are made by vampires:
Just as a mythical vampire is created as a result of being victim to a vampire, so it is with energy vampires. When the vampire bites into the neck of a victim, that victim begins a slow transformation into vampire, becoming more and more a creature of the night.

Energy vampires are usually victims of vampires, perhaps a 'vampiric' parent, sibling or friend can cause the vampire within us to rise from the grave. It is typical for the process of vampirism to create an almost instant hunger in the victim.

In order that we may become able to move into a new way of being, we need first to slay our own vampire, and then, deal with energy vampirism from others.

How do we know when our vampire has risen from the grave?
Identify the behaviours you use to get what you want. How often do you clearly state your needs? For many people the tactic considered most effective is covert manipulation rather than overtly stating needs.

Consider the following example Fig 4.1:

Fig 4.1 Vampiric Exchange—Example

A: (Just arrived home from work) I've had such a hectic day, I am exhausted.
      I suppose I had better get the dinner ready now.

B: I've had a busy day too. I thought I would put my feet up.

A: I would love to be able to put my feet up, but I have to get the dinner.

B: Would you like me to help you?

A: Oh no, I'll do it, don't worry about me. I can manage, it is my turn tonight, after all, I don't want to take advantage.....

B: Its not taking advantage, why don't I do it for you. I've had a bit of a rest.

A: No, no, I'll be alright (putting hand on back to indicate back strain).

B: Look, you go and take a bath, I'll make the dinner.

A: Are you sure?

B: Of course, don't worry about it, I'm more than happy to do it.

A: Well, if you are sure....

What is happening?

A is using vampirism on B. A should clearly state his/her needs, rather than use vampirism to exert control. B will feel exhausted by the exchange and probably aggrieved about it later.

What happens afterwards?

For many of us, manipulation is an effective way of achieving our ends. We want to receive love and care from the people we love or from those with whom we work. However, we frequently fail to ask for the simple things that these people are more than happy to give to us.

We tend to find ourselves activating our vampires as a direct result of energy loss. For example, when we have just been victim to a vampire we tend to find someone onto whom we can unburden ourselves. Thus we become a vampire.

We need to recognise when the flow of energy is coming towards us without it returning to another. In other words, what do we tend to do to gather an influx of energy? What are our tactics?

The Energy Vacuum:

Vampirism creates an energy vacuum and we are driven immediately to replenish our missing energy.

When we are drained of energy it is like an instant hunger. We do not feel the usual hunger pangs that we feel when we have a hunger for food. Instead this hunger works like a vacuum. Whenever a vacuum occurs matter seeks to fill it immediately as nature abhors a vacuum.

Pure vacuums are rare and in nature an example of a partial vacuum can be seen in weather systems. If seen in three dimensions, a low-pressure area is like a valley in the hillside of a high-pressure zone. The rising warm air of the high pressure "hills" draw air upwards creating a notional doughnut shaped "hole" in the air and the high pressure rushes to fill this "valley". The rapid movement of air causes winds that at their most extreme can be violent storms.

This process can be seen in the vampire's victim. The hole that the energy loss creates demands that it is filled, and the energy will be taken from the nearest available source. The process of ingestion of energy by the vampire can be a violent one, as the vampire makes its immediate demands upon the new victim. The filling of the vacuum creates a level of unconscious manipulation in the vampire that could be inconceivable to its conscious mind.

As the winds rush into the hole that has been punched in the atmosphere, so the vampire finds the release valve that will allow the energy to flow back into itself, so that the vacuum is refilled.

Energy that is stolen is limited. This is obvious because it can only be gained from the original source, the victim, and therefore we only have access to it when the victim is either close to us, or communicating with us. Energy we draw from the universe is unlimited as it depends only upon our ability to connect with what is freely available to all. As long as we remain connected we

Fig 4.2 **Are you filling an Energy Vacuum?**
Quick Quiz:

If you answer yes to any of the following, then you have probably used vampirism. If you answer "yes" you may be substituting power for love. Read the chapter to see how to cure these tendencies.

	Yes	No
1. Do you find yourself becoming a martyr to get your own way?		
2. Do you feel energised when you have told someone your problems?		
3. Do you find people "don't understand how you feel"?		
4. Are you often too tired to "make an effort" with friends?		
5. Do you use piercing looks to get your own way, or stomp and blast people?		
6. Do you complain that you are not appreciated and make noises that encourage others to give you support?		

can gain all we need. In Chapter 5 we consider how to do this in detail.

When we remain connected to this unlimited source of energy, we do not have to fear the effects of the vampire. However, our problem is in preventing ourselves from allowing our own vampire to rise, and unless we do so, we will continue to create vacuums in ourselves and in others.

Nests of Vampires:

"The Firm" a novel by John Grisham demonstrates how a nest of vampires can come about. Each new generation of young lawyers that come into the firm join the "nest" of Advisor and Corrupter vampires. There are layers of vampires in this story, each mentor feeding off its subordinate victim until the victim becomes a vampire and does the same. The victims learn how to drink in the life of the vampire without any remorse. This extends to the home life and marriages of the victims, who become sexually corrupted, taking lovers and punishing marriages.

Fig 4.3 **The Stages of Intoxication:** **Stage 4—The Transformation**		
Stages	**What is happening**	**How you are feeling**
6. The Persistent Vacuum	The re-occurring process of energy loss leaves a vacuum that cannot be replaced by further vampirism.	Returning to have yet more energy sucked only makes the feeling of dissatisfaction worse for the victim, even though the desire to be vampirised is still great.
9. The Quick Fix	Having been vampirised the victim immediately searches for a way to replenish the energy vacuum	The victim feels the need for reassurance, support or affection.
10. The Transformation	The victim, now transformed into vampire, finds a suitable person from whom energy can be drained.	Without realising it, victim has become vampire. The victim will be unaware that the inevitable transformation has taken place.

Fig 4.4 **How the process of transformation can occur**			
Hidden Vampirism	**Immediate and Apparent Response**	**Actual Transformation as a result of Energy Vacuum**	**How you may feel when you become aware of the Energy Theft**
A friend calls and unburdens himself upon you, telling you about his problems at work.	Following the call you feel tired and decide to call your mother.	You have a good moan about your friend.	Anger with friend.
You get "blasted" by your boss.	You capitulate, and behave meekly.	You shout at your partner when you get home.	You feel aggrieved.
Your partner tells you s/he is feeling poorly but is happy to go and get the shopping. You intervene and say you will do it instead.	You feel you must be kind to your partner when s/he feels like this.	When you arrive at the Supermarket you make such a fuss about loading the goods that a member of staff offers to help. You eventually accept help, after making many (but not too many) remonstrations to the contrary.	You feel guilty and put upon at the same time.
Your boss tells you that you could be considered for promotion, but that unless you were seen to be more willing to put in extra hours you would probably be passed over.	You realise that this must look very bad, and that you need to alter your behaviour immediately.	You tell your partner, unsympathetically, that he or she will have to put up with the additional hours, after all, you are only doing this for him/her.	You feel annoyed that you have not been appreciated for what you have done and for who you are.

In the film adaptation of the book, Tom Cruise plays a young, newly qualified, lawyer, Mitch McDeere, a potential high flyer who is sought after by many big firms, but eventually is wooed by a "family" firm in Memphis, Tennessee. Mitch's wife Abby (Jeanne Tripplehorn) is suspicious, because the firm has such rigid code of practice for its staff, including how they live their domestic life.

Mitch throws himself into his work, and curries favour with his boss, and lunches with his mentor Avery Tolar (Gene Hackman), listening to his wisdom and absorbing the culture. Abby continues to feel alienated by it.

The relationship between Mitch and his wife Abby is on a knife edge particularly after Mitch is set up and tempted into sex with an unknown girl on a beach in the Cayman Islands. His immediate remorse is irrelevant, as the event is used to control him, with photos of the event sent to Abby. The relationship between Mitch and Abby becomes unstable and Avery joins the picture, attempting to seduce Abby.

Avery's eventual demise is (metaphorically) typical of the Corrupter Vampire. Feeling there is no way out of his life of vampirism, he explains to Abby how he was lured into the life and is unable to find any release or liberation from it. He tells her about the woman he loved and how he lost her, with intense regret, but does not see any escape. Finally, he kills himself.

This story illustrates vampirism on many different levels, and demonstrates the Corrupter Vampire perfectly. The Nest of Vampires calls itself a Family, and has strict codes, typical of Corrupter Vampires, because they like to control everything and everyone around them.

It is interesting to see how the vampire chain extends from Mitch's boss, through his mentor to him, and ultimately how this infects his wife. It is typical that a Corrupter Vampire mixes sex and power, they will often have affairs or flirt and sexually manipulate their "prey", sometimes through relentless pursuit and often this is, in reality, sexual harassment. The victims of the harassment rarely take any action, legal or otherwise, to stop it.

Nests of Vampires within the Family:

Although nests of vampires may be pernicious in the workplace, frequently they are seen within the family. As vampires are usually created within us as a result of our tactics as children, it is not surprising that we may find vampires residing with us at home.

Many situation comedies are based upon this concept, whereby the maternal vampires are often the mothers, using guilt to wield power—consider American Situation Comedy "Roseanne". The title character, played by Roseanne Barr,

Fig 4.5 **Are there Vampires in the family?**
Quick Quiz:

If you answer yes to any of the following, then beware, the vampire may be residing at your house! The following are typical vampire behaviours that may be found in the home:

	Yes	No
1. In order to get anything done, nagging is required. *If yes, this may be the tactics of Intimidating Vampires, or sometimes Guilt Vampires can nag, but it will be very subtle!*		
2. Because the family do not contribute, it is necessary to do everything yourself, whilst quietly moaning. *If yes, this may be the Guilt Vampire.*		
3. Sarcasm is used frequently. *If yes, this may be the Intimidating Vampire who may use sarcasm, as it is a form of aggressive assertion. However, it can be a Charismatic Vampire that may use it as vampirising "humour".*		
4. Competition exists between family members, each trying to out do the other in criticising each others interests, music, friends etc *If yes, a maelstrom of vampire types could be involved here.*		
5. Parents provide a united front, and children complain that their point of view is not "heard" or considered of value; "Mum and Dad know best". *If yes, "Mum and Dad" could be Advisor Vampires.*		
6. One individual criticises and complains about another to a third member. *If yes, a Corrupter Vampire enticing others to join his/her campaign*		
7. Members can be made to feel guilty quite easily. *If yes, probably a Guilt Vampires; however, it can also be used effectively by Needy Vampires*		
8. Everyone picks on the little one. *If yes, there may be a mixture of possible vampire types, but everyone picking on one member is typical of "Vampire Nest" behaviour, the little one being at the bottom of the pecking order and therefore easy "meat".*		
9. The ones that complain that "It's not fair" receive "special" treatment in order to help them to feel equal. *If yes, this may be Needy Vampires at work.*		
10. One member of the family is a "tour de force" and tends to have most of the influence. *If yes, this may be a Charismatic Vampire who is suffocating the others.*		

has a vampiric mother herself, and vampirises her own children with her cutting humour. Although funny, it is damaging if it gives the impression that this is clever and effective parenting; the vampire mother gaining the power from being perceived as smart and witty at the expense of the children and partner (in this case her husband).

In this particular Situation Comedy every member of the family vies for power, and, although the programme tries to demonstrate a loving family life, this end message is given as "I vampirise you because I love you".

This format is used extensively in Situational Comedies, and in recent television programmes such as "My Family" on BBC 1, the same formula is used with vampiristic children and parents, each attempting to be the one who "wins the power".

The questionnaire highlights only a few examples of vampirism in the family. However, if we are to improve our relationships in life, what better place to start than at home. We need to be able to recognise these behaviours before we can change them.

Nests of Vampires within Friendship Groups:

It is not uncommon for vampires to exist within friendship groups. The same kinds of nests may exist, with certain friends exerting power over others. A classic example of this: Friend A to Friend B: Don't tell Friend C but....".

In this case Friend A may be expecting B to keep a confidence that is not in the best interests of Friend C. However, if you tell C you are letting down A. This kind of manipulative behaviour will create pushes and pulls of energy within the group and ultimately make the relationships exhausting.

All the strategies used by the different vampires are likely to be seen in nests according to the individual and how the vampire may become manifest within him or her.

The Advisor Vampire

How to lose the Vampire Lifestyle.

Vampires live in The House of Horrors. Without realising it we may be "walking with the undead". This means recognising the things that we do and say that prevent us from breaking out of this House of Horrors and living in the "joyful light". In order to create joy in our lives we need to create a world for ourselves in which joy can thrive.

Trying to keep out pain, but actually keeping it in:

We think that the walls of the House of Horrors will keep us protected from the outside, but instead they retain every imaginable misery within. Here, rooms remain the same, year after year, with never the sunlight of joy being shone upon them. We revel in picking up and turning in our hands our old wounds and hurts. And when we grow tired of this, we immerse ourselves in all the sadness and pain the world can offer.

Paradigms—Living in a painful and negative world:

How do you live your life? Your paradigm (pronounced para-dime) is your personal view of the world in which you live; how you see life. We each have different ways of perceiving the same events; this depends upon our paradigm. And each of us has a unique paradigm, because no one else can see quite what we see when we look at life. In what paradigm do you live? What is the world like from where you stand?

The House of Horrors is a way of describing a paradigm of the world that many of us share. In other words, do you surround yourself with negativism? If so, you are creating a reality for yourself that is uncomfortable and that will naturally create negativity in your relationships. Before you can find joy in your life you need to be creating a world in which joy can thrive.

Patch Adams is best known as the red-nosed doctor, brought to fame by Robin Williams's portrayal of him in the film "Patch Adams". He feels that this dark world in which we live in is a function of a competitive patriarchal world. He believes that the male-dominated, hierarchical government systems tend to create struggles for power and status, at the expense of brother- and sister-hood, caring and support.

Feminine principles are more likely to lead to a mutually caring and understanding system, but the toppling of society is not likely to be effected without a fight, and the male principle still lives on.

We can change the world by changing ourselves, because it is us who are the world, and while we maintain the House of Horrors, it will continue to exist, and we within it, although this is not really living.

Fig 4.6 Are You Living in the House of Horrors or the Sunshine of Joy?
Quick Quiz:

If you answer yes to any of the following, then you are noticing symptoms that indicate that you may be living in the House of Horrors.
Read the chapter to rediscover the Joy Paradigm.

Do you:	Yes	No
1. Follow tragic stories in the paper, such as Murder Trials etc?		
2. Watch Soap Operas on TV?		
3. Make sure you watch the News everyday, usually last thing at night?		
4. Criticise the rich and famous?		
5. Talk about people you do not approve of, and make your opinions known to others?		
6. Spend money you do not have, such as on credit cards?		
7. Gossip, spread rumours or make assumptions about people based upon what you hear?		
8. Like watching films about disaster, murder, rape, evil and supernatural thrillers and other misery dramas etc?		
9. Notice how messy and dirty your environment is?		
10. Spend most of your life eating food you do not like because you are on a diet?		
11. Drink alcohol in order to enjoy yourself and/or smoke to get yourself going in the mornings?		
12. Think that any young people you see in the street are probably up to "no good"?		
13. Fear that there are many "weird" people out there and prevent your children from going out alone, feel suspicious of people who smile and say hello, imagine that people are breaking the law or doing nasty things even in your own locality.		
14. Use sarcasm or shout at the children.		

The House of Horrors:

The House of Horrors is typified by behaviours that reinforce stereotypes and underline tragedies. It is sad, but also true, that many of us find our common ground with others by living within the House of Horrors. We pass the time by talking about the latest tragedy in the newspaper, we complain about the state of the roads, the health service, the "youth". We notice the bad things in our community, the litter, the graffiti, the vandalism.

We spend time talking about political issues, because we want to complain about the way things are; the law is unfair, politicians are corrupt, none of us feel safe.

We tell each other tales, often urban myths, about the cruelty and evil that one person will do unto another; children stolen and sold, murder, mayhem, abuse.

We trade stories with each other on how awful our parents are, how badly we were brought up, how screwed up we are by other people.

Then we relax in front of the television and watch soap operas that are full of shouting people, broken marriages, rejected children, violence, swearing, misery and aggression. Or put on some sport and shout and jibe at the players when they are failing to score, or, when they do, celebrate the success of these people who we do not know as though it were our own.

Perhaps for a change we will watch a fly on the wall documentary, discovering how tedious other people's lives are, and yet becoming embroiled in the pseudo stars lives, picking up the tabloids to see whether they have managed to sort out their problems, or whether they are now presenting a children's programme on Satellite TV.

For a treat we may go to the cinema and see the latest blockbuster; disaster, end of the world, corruption in government, war, evil, supernatural forces, broken relationships, mistrust, murder and death. Loss of life is a part of almost every film made in Hollywood, and not just one, but many, anonymous faces dying horrible deaths.

When we read the press or a magazine we are drawn to true-life dramas, the film star who has an alcohol problem, the pregnant pop singer who has broken up with her boyfriend.

When we are not talking about the rich and famous, we are talking about the people we know, we spread rumour and innuendo, we judge and criticise. We go home and find our own lives lacking in sparkle. We feel old and blame this upon our partners, we criticise them to their face or behind their backs.

Perhaps we look for excitement elsewhere, maybe having sex with people we don't know and then feeling cheap and unhappy. To feel better about ourselves we publicise our conquests as though this will increase our self worth, whilst it devalues the other person.

We put the radio on and listen to music that tells us of loss, misery and depression, that speaks about addiction and anger. Our friends come round to see us and we talk about how men/women are the bane of our life, to complain that we have been mistreated and to drown our sorrows. That is when we can be bothered to see our friends, because most of the time we do not have the energy to get off the sofa.

To "sooth our nerves" we take out a bottle and pour some alcohol into our own glass, it helps us to feel better about the lousy day we had at work, the fact that we forgot to visit the school about our children's problems and to forget that we are alone.

This is the House of Horrors. And that is quite enough of all that! Someone open the curtains immediately!

Recognising that we live in the House of Horrors:
You are presumably reading this book because you want to find new ways of being, and not because you want to remind yourself of all those things that are a part of the House of Horrors. However, we do need to consider the meaning of this in our lives if we are going to make positive changes.

Perhaps you do not recognise some elements of the House of Horrors, but you may recognise many. Consider the questionnaire and see if you are living within the House of Horrors. If you are then the first thing you need to do is shift this paradigm of life.

When we realise that we live with pain we can begin to alter this and create a new paradigm for ourselves.

How does our paradigm affect our lives?
When we live within the House of Horrors, we make it our reality. In other words, we live with pain constantly and pain becomes our way of being. The House of Horrors suffocates us and drains us of our energy. It is easy to vampirise someone who is existing within the House of Horrors. They are already vulnerable, they are looking for reasons for their suffering, and they are happy to latch onto another person for support. When we are in the House of Horrors we are Vampires waiting to bite.

Sex, Sexuality and Gender:
I am not suggesting that men are a certain way and women another. Although some writers like to draw clear distinctions between men and women and their

respective behaviours, which may resonate with readers to a greater or lesser degree, I prefer to work from the basis that an individual has his or her own ways of being. This may be somewhat clouded by gender and sex, but not necessarily.

When we consider sex as the defining characteristic, we exclude the many millions who do not conform to the limiting role that this imposes. In fact, who is to say that any of us truly fit the narrow definitions of maleness or femaleness. Gay couples, transsexuals, transvestites are a few of the many ways in which gender and sexuality may be expressed. Theoretically, there is much more acceptability of differences in sexuality and gender. Reality may not be as comforting.

So you think the media does not affect you? Think again!

Cosmopolitan Magazine did an interesting article to test perceptions of female body shape. They took about six different body types, and pictured them in the same leotard with the same face stuck on. They then asked people which was their most preferred.

Almost without exception the men and women pointed to the thin, tall model. I was surprised that everyone really did find her the most attractive. However, at first look, she embodied everything the media has been telling us for years is perfection in the female form. But so thin! What shocked me was that you see one woman like this in a hundred; so why are we all yearning to be like, or to be with a woman that is not representative of women?

If you love women, then surely it is the womanliness that you love. This is represented in as many different ways as there are women on earth. Why do we narrow down to one, media created type? This is not a criticism of tall and thin women, but *only to* see this as beautiful is, itself, unnatural.

I wanted to test the Cosmopolitan findings myself, and so used my husband! Which one did he find most attractive? Shock and horror, it was the same one, the tall and thin. Considering that I am *not* tall and I am *not* thin was a little disconcerting. So I asked him to tell me why he chose this one. "Well", he said with a pleased look on his face, "That is the one that looks most like you!"

Hmm.. "But," I protested, "She doesn't look anything like me; notice first the height, she six foot, me five foot four. Notice second the fact that I could get two of her inside my trousers (presumably one in each leg). Notice third, that the body shape two to the right of this one is almost perfectly me (a squarer, stocky and shorter body—and I am totally happy with it)!"

My husband looked from one to the other, from thin and tall to square and stocky. "You're right!" he said with a hint of "eureka!" in his voice. In fact, he went on to say, that when he looked closely, and with new insight, he realised that tall and bony was not at all attractive to him.

So why did he choose it then? Our conclusion—it is not his fault. He is a victim of the media. He has been sold an ideal of beauty from TV, film, advertising; we are all bombarded night and day. So much so that his brain was connecting thin and tall to beauty, so that the image lied to him. It lied that this was what he found attractive, and as he finds me attractive, it lied to him that I was this woman.

I am lucky that my husband thinks that I am his ideal mate. But then, perhaps many more people would realise that their ideal mate is the one with whom they are with right now, and that comparison and competition are media tools that are used for one reason only; to sell something.

Manipulating your insecurities:

The advertising media works by playing on your insecurities. Are you afraid of being lonely? Penniless? Ugly? Old? Unloved? Whatever it is, advertising will play upon it to wield power over you.

Advertising is also one of the most creative, entertaining and innovative media we have. Enjoy advertising. Learn from it. Make judgements based upon what is right for you. Know when you are being vampirised, and let go of perfection. Every soul is perfect no matter what packaging it comes in. Because we are each unique, we cannot compare one to another. A rose is as beautiful as a daisy, although they are different.

Danger and Instincts:

There are so many situations, these days, where we feel threatened that we often avoid venturing out into the world and sharing with others. We attempt to protect our children from everything, and treat life as though it has a guarantee attached, rather than a warning.

By assuming everything and everyone is a threat we shut ourselves off from our instincts and from our ability to tap into true companionship. We look for evil, and so we find it, which is demonstrated in the adage "Where the attention goes, the energy flows". In other words, the things upon which we focus become true for us. For example, if we focus upon our debts they become greater, but if we focus on our wealth it grows instead.

How often do people quote Murphy's Law? That is, "If something can possibly go wrong, then it will!" The more we are putting our attention upon the things that can fail, the less we keep our eye on what we should be doing to be a success. For instance, when driving a car, if you look at the dangers you tend to drive at them: if you stare at the car in front, you can end up driving straight into its rear.

Likewise, trying to tell ourselves not to do something has the opposite effect. When we say "I must not do..." or "I will not..." our subconscious removes the word "not" and we find ourselves helplessly doing the very thing we want to avoid.

For example, I was cooking an omelette and put the skillet in the oven to finish it off. As I removed it with my oven glove I told myself "don't forget to use the oven glove", over and over again as I proceeded with other tasks around the kitchen. When I went back to the pan I put my hand directly on the handle without an oven glove on and burnt it.

We are programmed to see danger in everything. When we read the papers or hear the News we are primarily exposed to the negative things taking place: disaster, murder and mayhem. This leads us to believe that these are around every corner. This suspicion makes us afraid to open up to people and commit to companionship and friendship. We end up relying on having our friends and lovers "screened" by using dating agencies or small ads, by relying on others to introduce us to new people.

This prevents a free flow of energy and makes us perfect victims of vampires. Vampires are extremely clever at appearing to be harmless and having our interests at heart. They use the fact that we are afraid to lull us into a false security, where they can happily prey upon us. We end up turning to the vampire for help, and believing it will be our protector.

It is essential that we open ourselves up to life by accepting that there is a risk, and that this is a part of the ebb and flow of energy that is around us. By doing so we activate our instincts, and then we *know* when we are faced with real danger, and not the imagined danger we see in every face.

We must rely upon our instincts, and act upon them. When we feel a danger, we must believe it, and take immediate action. When we do not detect this danger we can "go with the flow" trusting ourselves at every step and making decisions based strongly upon our intuition.

When you enter the Sunshine of Joy you do not need to be on the look out for vampires. On the one hand, you will notice and handle potential vampirism without the need to think consciously about it, and on the other hand you will find you stop attracting vampires into your life, as they know they will be denied a feed. This may have an affect on your relationships. I have known many vampires who have taken a "dislike" to me when I have given them no reason whatsoever. On the surface they have remained friendly and charming, but have clearly felt disorientated by me, and have told other people that I have never liked them!

In the two particular cases I recall, the vampires were the husbands of friends of mine. The women both noticed the reaction of their husbands and mentioned it to me, they described the reason they believed their men were wary as being due to my "seeing through them". In both cases the women were badly vampirised by their husbands and both eventually left them.

There is no reason to feel disappointed about some people not liking you. Do you really want to be on friendly terms with a vampire, knowing, as we do, that they are interested in one thing only?

Sleepwalking our way through life:

When we live within the House of Horrors we can be described as in a somnambulistic state, in other words, we are sleepwalking. We are not awake to reality, to beauty or to faith in human nature. When we are sleepwalking we are very easily suggestible. It is like we are in a state of partial hypnosis, when we hear a news story, or hear a vampire telling us stories of crimes and misdemeanours that are going on under our own noses, we believe them implicitly. When we read a story in the press, even though we know the source is not wholly reputable, we believe it.

Rumour becomes true for us, because it is in print, because someone we know speaks it. We fail to lend any balanced judgement, we respond. And our response is also suggested; in our sleepwalking state we respond with the requisite shock, disgust, and plenty of judgement. We are quick to point out that only a thoroughly reprehensible person would do such as thing; that in his/her position, we would never do that, we would be dignified, kind, upstanding etc.

In a somnambulistic state we see only what it is suggested that we see. We hear only what it is suggested that we hear. We miss out on the richness of life, the many different coloured threads that pull our world together into a whole tapestry of experience and vitality. We miss the "unimportant things" because in our "suggested" state we are blind and deaf to them. These unimportant things are the joys in life, because the House of Horrors is nothing if not self-perpetuating, and when we begin to realise that good news is more sustaining that bad news we may no longer wish to be a part of that dark world.

So we are sleep walking, and if we are to see the true beauty we need to shake ourselves awake.

Retreating to the coffin:

Like Dracula we may think that we are interacting with the world, but our journeys outside may be only to feed our pain with more pain. And when we become tired and disillusioned we retreat further into our coffin and shut the lid.

Here we lay on the soil of our homeland, in other words, we retreat into an illusion of how the world should be, our dreams of an idyllic life, maybe that were sown in our childhood. We shut our eyes "knowing" that this is simply a flight of fancy, and that when we awaken we will once more be within our dark castle.

When we are in our coffin we are trying to escape from life by setting up an illusion, which gives us a short term boost, but from which we will fall deeper into pain in the end. Perhaps we go out and "drown our sorrows" with excess alcohol, or, when having financial difficulties, spend a load of money on our credit card to buy a holiday, not considering how we are to pay it back afterwards. In both cases we are escaping only temporarily from the problems and we create even greater ones in the end.

Forgiveness as the key:

To quote "A Course in Miracles"- "Forgiveness offers everything I want:

"What could you want that forgiveness cannot give? Do you want peace? Forgiveness offers it. Do you want happiness, a quiet mind, a certainty of purpose, and a sense of worth and beauty that transcend the world? Do you want care and safety and the warmth of sure protection always? Do you want a quietness that cannot be disturbed, a gentleness that can never be hurt, a deep abiding comfort, and a rest so perfect it can never be upset?

"All this forgiveness offers you and more. It sparkles on your eyes as you awake, and gives you joy with which to meet the day. It soothes your forehead while you sleep, and rests upon your eyelids so you see no dreams of fear and evil, malice and attack. And when you wake again, it offers you another day of happiness and peace. All this forgiveness offers you, and more."

The moment you stop yourself, whether before you speak, mid sentence, or immediately afterwards, notice your behaviour, correct it and explain why you are re-enacting the situation, you will realise that you have been able to forgive yourself, rather than pretend that you have been a victim and not a vampire.

Even if another vampire caused your own to rise from the grave, you will still feel forgiven by yourself and by your partner. You will find a great sense of peace in your communication, and you will not feel under pressure to "get things right" all the time. Instead, you find that when you do not "get things right" the situation becomes right, and in a more powerful way than before.

Opening up the House of Horrors:

In order to get back into the sunshine, we need to become aware of drifting into the House of Horrors, so that we can prevent ourselves from living the Vampire's Lifestyle.

When we forgive, and when this is genuine and from the heart, we immediately replenish ourselves with energy and the result is synergy for both partners (in other words, both get more out than they put in) and both partners feel renewed and refreshed.

See the steps in fig. 4.8. This process teaches our communication partner how to forgive, and at the same time we learn how to forgive him or her, and ourselves.

I am never upset for the reason I think:

When we try to forgive we can sometimes find it difficult because we are not upset for the reasons we think. Does this surprise you?

Well try testing this idea. Firstly accept that it is true, and then, every time you are upset say to yourself, "I am not upset for the reason I think". You may then find that thoughts and ideas drift up from you subconscious and enlighten you with greater wisdom, although I cannot say whether you will reach any firm conclusions.

How do we know that we are never upset for the reasons we think? Well, think about a time when your partner or a close friend asked for forgiveness and you found it difficult to grant. Why was it so difficult to say, "I forgive"?

Perhaps you found that you manipulated further and further as your partner tried to ask for forgiveness, as you were never satisfied that he or she was sufficiently sorry.

If you were really upset for the reasons you thought you would have accepted that apology immediately. When the apology sticks in our throats, it is because it is not curing, and that is because we are placing the "cure" on the outside of us, expecting someone else to have the answer.

Vampires feed off resentment and when an old wound is opened by accident or deliberately by another, the vampire within us can want to take control. If we accept that we are not upset for the reason we think we are then we will be allowing the true feelings to surface and we can also accept the role the inner vampire is playing in manipulating our loved ones and us.

Fig 4.7i **Are You Living in the House of Horrors or the Sunshine of Joy? Answers:**	
Note the question numbers you ticked and then read the information below that may explain why your answers suggest that you may be living in the House of Horrors.	
Note the numbers you ticked and then read the notes below:	Yes
1. Newspapers: We can become over involved in the negative things in life. The News rarely tells us anything happy to celebrate; by watching the bad and the sad we may begin to believe that life is really like that. But it is only like that rarely and for a very few people. It is all about balance. How much news can you usefully process? I think many of us believe we have a duty to share the suffering of another, and that by doing so we subconsciously prevent the same tragedy from happening to us. Of course, this is not true. Our life will take its own path, and although we can influence it as much as possible, the final result is indeterminable.	✓
2. Soap Operas: Soaps are often (though not invariably) based upon tragedy. Is our soap a happy tale or is it a miserable mixture of deception, crime, broken relationships and unhappy lives? The world of the soap is usually firmly based upon the House of Horrors. It is easier to be entertaining by inventing more and more bizarre and tear-jerking storylines than it is to maintain public interest with a story of happy people who do happy things every day of their lives. Sad but true. People will switch channels if the story is dull, but people will continue to watch tales of woe no matter how tedious the story line. And they are tedious, a soap promises a big showdown and yet you have to wait weeks and weeks while they stretch out the story to keep you hanging on, and on and on. If all this sounds a lot like vampirism then you are right! Notice the way you feel after the soap. Do you talk about it to friends and colleagues? Does it almost seem real to you? Do you talk about the actors by their characters' names? Are you being drawn into this world of misery? Resist! Happiness can be interesting, and it is laziness on the part of scriptwriters to create nothing but shock and misery. Fight the vampire by ignoring him. The angel is waiting patiently for you begin to show an interest!	✓
3. News: See 1. Above. Watching the News last thing at night is not good for peace of mind at bedtime.	✓

Fig 4.7ii	
4. Criticism of the Rich and Famous The House of Horrors encourages criticism. This is because we focus on the "outside" and not on the "inside" of ourselves. We are busy looking at what other people are doing, and how we could be so much better than they. Take for instance a film star who has cosmetic surgery. We all sit around with an opinion about it, saying what we would do in his/her place. The truth is, we do not know what we would do in his/her place, and it is pointless to speculate. Perhaps we are a little envious about the money he or she has, and we want to imagine how we could spend it better. The House of Horrors is a place where we never have enough, and so when we see others who have enough we do not believe that they deserve it; we are jealous or critical. In the Sunshine of Joy we say "Good for you" and "That's something I would like too—well done you!" In the Sunshine of Joy there is enough for all of us.	✓
5. Criticism of Others See 4. Above. Why focus on them? Are we deflecting our attention from ourselves? We do not need to compare ourselves to others in order to feel good. The expression "Physician heal thyself" comes to mind. In other words, before "curing" everyone else, put your own life properly in order! It is commonplace when you read a book that has some useful insights on life, to want to share it with others. This is wonderful, but please remember, before you put them to rights, sort yourself out!	✓
6. Money: Borrowing and borrowing is storing up problems to gripe about later—spending money does not make you feel better– it is a temporary high, and as such it cannot be classified as a true lifter. Just like drinking and drugs. Happiness is not commercialism, the best things in life **are** free. When you feel the impulse for some retail therapy remember that you are sinking into the House of Horrors. You are putting yourself at the mercy of events that will set you up for a calamitous fall. Kick the habit! When I have had my times of deepest financial gloom, and I have telephoned my parents to gripe, I realise quite quickly that, actually it is not such as big deal. It feels like it at the time, but, if you face it, it no longer has the power to control and drain you. Like the vampire, financial stresses like to lurk in the shadows. As soon as they are in the open their power to terrorise is neutralised. Even when I have been penniless with many wolves baying for blood at my door, and I have felt that there was no where left to turn, a number of truths hit me. Firstly, I would survive it. Secondly, bricks and mortar are not life and limb, and we attach too much meaning to them. Thirdly, my happiness is a function of my state of mind, not my state of wealth. Fourthly, my state of wealth is a result of my state of mind.	✓

Fig 4.7iii	
7. Gossip and Rumour Gossip is just a way of spreading insecurity and enjoying others' misfortune. Rumour mongering is tantamount to telling lies—ignorance of the truth is no excuse for flouting it. We have the power to alter reality and make rumour become truth. Gossips are also blind. They think no one knows what they are saying behind their hands, but the subject of the gossip is only too well aware; but what shall they do? Should they point out that they know about the rumours and deny them? That would strengthen the Gossips case! Or ignore them. That gives the Gossips carte blanche to continue. Gossips may think it is harmless but in fact they are causing hurt and suffering, undermining relationships and destroying lives. In the House of Horrors we enjoy misery, particularly for others; in the Sunshine of Joy we do not have time for it, because we are having too much fun. Gossiping thrives on misery and is vampirism. Spending time with others in the Sunshine of Joy is to be truly intimate; in other words, to find out about the real person within. Then we can see the shining light, the angel, that is within. Rumour, gossip and innuendo deal with falsely constructed views of others. Let's get into intimacy and relate to them. We are all worthy of that.	✓
8. Films: How many films do you see in which someone dies? How many people die? More than one? More than ten? Maybe more than one hundred? The affects of TV violence have been studied and it is shocking to notice how much of our viewing has some allusion to violence. Various studies have shown that children are more likely to behave violently after they have seen violence on the TV, that even violence committed for "good" reasons is likely to make them more hostile. TV Violence also provides children with new and original ways of being aggressive. How does this affect adults? Well we think that we are unaffected, as we are able to process the information from film and TV in a mature and adult manner. We "know" that we are unaffected because we notice that we do not immediately commit an act of violence following a violent show on TV or film. However, perhaps we do change our way of behaving slightly. Perhaps we are more likely to raise our voices, to be short tempered, to have an aggressive outburst, such as shouting or rudeness. Perhaps we feel a little less positive, a little more downcast. I believe that this is true, as I believe TV and film violence are draining forces. They vampirise us. Whereas, uplifting film and TV tends to fill us with the energy of joy and satisfaction.	✓

Fig 4.7iv	
9. Environment: Actually the world is full of beauty. Try noticing it. It is true that there are many sad sights; landfills, power stations, litter etc. But when we lift our heads to the heavens we see more than this, we can see the sun rise and set casting glorious yellows, reds, oranges and purples into the sky. We see the birds swooping and calling, the chatter of starlings, the chirruping of robins in the garden, the heart-breaking song of the thrush. We can see the watery haze that makes our English landscape so breathtakingly beautiful, and notice the vivid brightness that makes a New York sky so wholesome and engaging. We begin to see the trees, the bark, the lichen. We hear sounds we have never heard before (but they were always calling to us), the owl hooting, the fox barking, the outrageous noise of a gang of badgers. We can hear the distant cries and yells of delight from children at a nearby school. We can feel the sun, as it breaks through a cloud warming our shoulders. For every sight that saddens, there are a million to thrill. Allow the cold vampire heart to be warmed by nature in all its many glorious forms.	✓
10. Dieting: The House of Horrors says health is no fun. The Sunshine of Joy says—have fun, and you will be healthy! We spend so much time looking at ourselves critically, we fail to see the real person behind the mask. The vampire in us is at work when we hear all that self criticism. The vampire in the media is at work when we see picture of unnaturally thin models and think that this is the standard against which we must set ourselves. In the House of Horrors we are struggling against our natures. In the Sunshine of Joy we are in love with who we are. We recognise that it is our uniqueness that makes us important and special.	✓
11. Drinking/Smoking/Drugs Are drinking alcohol, smoking and/or taking drugs really part of the House of Horrors? Narcotics in any form can vampirise you. The narcotic itself is inert, but the circumstances around it make it dangerous. Most things are relatively safe in moderation. Anything and everything can be dangerous when in excess, or when you rely upon it. When you consume alcohol or drugs to alter your perceptions then it is a danger to you regardless of how much or how little you take. In the Sunshine of Joy we may enjoy a good glass of wine, or an occasional cigarette because we like the flavour. However, when we say we drink/smoke to relax/get going/ concentrate/enjoy ourselves etc we are in the House of Horrors; the narcotic has vampirised us, it is influencing us. We need to withdraw from its power now. Get drunk on the beauty you see in the face of everyone who passes you in the street. Try smiling. See what response you get—remember that many people are still in the House of Horrors, they will see smiling as odd— "What have you got to be so pleased with yourself about?" However, you will also notice that most people will smile back. Remember, a smile is free to give, and yet priceless to receive.	✓

Fig 4.7v	
12. Young People: Most people are honest and good. Young people are no exception. If you are prejudiced against them, you will attract ignorant and unkind people to you whether young or old. How do adults become honest and good? They start off as honest and good young people. If youngsters are angry about the state of the world, then who can blame them? We made it, not them! And yet, look at the good that is done by the young everyday. They make our tomorrow, and we need to invest faith and trust in them, because children come into the world believing in Tellytubby land. Let's not force them into The House of Horrors, let's join them in Joy.	✓
13. Fear of People: Are things really worse today? I think we are more aware of the terrible things that can sometimes happen; we are informed about deaths and disasters, murders and abuse. What possible outcome can there be from this? We obsess about them. We become more interested and more concerned. We begin to create our world around these ideas. We make them a part of our reality. If we are to make a new and joyful world we cannot do so by concentrating upon negative thoughts. Our thoughts become our reality, so we need to start thinking positive thoughts now. Your first reaction to this maybe "what about the risk?" My answer is, don't take unnecessary risks, but at the same time, why do you prefer to assume that everyone is a threat? Use intuition. If you intuit something is not quite right, go with your feeling immediately. By the same token, learn to be more trusting. If we look for danger we will find it. Refer back to the section on TV and Film for more information.	✓
14. Sarcasm, shouting and other aggressive behaviour Sarcasm and shouting are aggression. Why are you shouting? Are you blaming your own tension upon the children? When we feel stressed by day-to-day living we have two options, to allow our children to pour the joy of their uncluttered lives upon us, or to shout at them. The former is surely more rewarding, and yet we so often infect their lives with our worldliness—"I am too busy" I just want to have a quiet drink" "Run along and play, would you?" Why are we sarcastic? It is a useful way of making a point aggressively under the guise of humour. It has been said that sarcasm is the lowest form of wit. Therefore, remember that to build and strengthen relationships with partners, children, colleagues or our boss we need to stop using sarcasm now.	✓

How to keep the vampire at bay.

We may be responsible for calling to the vampire to rise from the grave, but we must never invite it over the threshold of our home

Our responsibility to the vampire in others:

If we are being vampirised then we need to recognise our responsibility to this process. We have put ourselves in danger; we have made ourselves a target. Perhaps we have "invited the vampire in". For example, by providing a ready listening ear, or responding to manipulation we may encourage someone to vampirise us.

Steps	Fig 4.8 **Curing Your Communications of Vampirism**	
1	Awareness: Ask yourself "Has my inner vampire risen from the grave?"	Whenever you feel the vampire is at large in your relationships, look within first. Even if you feel the vampire is on the outside it will still indicate that your inner vampire is likely to have risen from the grave.
2	Assess your behaviours:	Before you can change yourself you need to know what you must change. Spot your vampiric attitudes, expressions and behaviours as soon as you have displayed them.
3	STOP and Apologise:	Immediately stop the vampiric behaviours and apologise for them.
4	Re-enact:	Restate the communication without the vampiric aspects. Although you have alerted your communication partner to your vampirism, by re-enacting you retain control over yourself, rather than allowing the inner vampire to continue to have power
5	Change:	By a slow process of change, you will find that you will automatically use vampiric behaviours less and less.
6	Forgiveness:	When you re-enact you will enable your communication partner to forgive your momentary vampirism, because it is easy to do so before it has created energy loss. Forgiveness is one of the greatest antidotes to Vampirism.

How can you protect yourself?

Vampires are not intentionally evil or cruel, a vampire is almost helpless in its use of manipulative means for achieving its aims. Remember a vampire is also a victim. However, we must still avoid becoming a victim, as this will lead us to becoming a vampire ourselves. Ultimately you cannot cure a vampire, a vampire needs to recognise itself in order to cure itself. However, you can protect yourself from predation.

While we are trying to protect ourselves from vampires, we may be unwittingly activating the vampire in others. This is very easily done, especially in loving relationships, so often, when we feel vampirised, we have no one to blame but ourselves.

However, you are safe within your own "home". Once you invite the vampire into your house, however, you are disempowered. Then, the vampire can rule over your domain.

Faith and The Cross::

Vampires can be warded off with The Cross, as this represents your faith. In the case of energy vampires this is not a religious faith, but your keeping faith with yourself, and not being led into the vampires' den by their manipulations.

Remain true to yourself at all costs, do not doubt what you see and hear. Hold your vision of what you believe and keep your intent pure. Believe in yourself and do not be side tracked by the vampire's machinations; do not allow the vampire to blind you to your brilliance, or to blast you into believing in your incompetence, to throw you off course and lead you "up the garden path".

Don't let it in!

We have to invite a vampire in, in order to become its victim. By being aware of a vampire we can avoid offering our throat to it. Once we have refused a vampire entry it cannot feed. This can frustrate it, and it may change behaviours and try new ways to lure you, but if you stand fast you will be safe.

You have to buy into the idea that it has power over you for it to succeed. When you realise that it does not have a hold unless you let it, you resume the power over yourself. Trust your instincts but do not forget to keep checking in with your consciousness. In this way, by simply becoming aware of vampirism, we automatically curtail it.

Ignore the Nonsense:

One way to avoid "letting the vampire in" is to use this simple strategy of "ignoring the nonsense". This means that we focus only on the message and not on the fluff or "violence" that goes with it. Consider when a person chooses to use their Intimidating Vampire to make a point. At work it may walk into your office waving a piece of paper (paper waving is a favourite tactic of Intimidating Vampires), shouting about mistakes that have been made. In this situation you should ignore everything that does not relate directly to the issue—so the shouting, waving, stomping, fist shaking - ignore it all.

Then listen. What is the real message? Respond to this and this alone. Ignore the rest (the nonsense as we call it, because it is all nonsense, and you do not need to buy into it). Answer the sensible points that are made, calmly, as though the anger and wild behaviour of the Intimidating Vampire had not occurred at all. You will find that most people who use their Intimidating Vampires in this way will run out of steam and quickly change tactics if this bullying does not work.

True Life Tales from the Crypt—Elizabeth:

Elizabeth realised that she had been the victim of a client who was a vampire. She decided "not to let it cross the threshold" and so when he next phoned her she kept this intent in mind. Quickly she realised that the vampire was behaving oddly, it even called her "dear" which was totally uncharacteristic. Afterwards Elizabeth felt really good, and not the usual energy depletion. She realised that the vampire was unable to "get its teeth in", so it changed tactic. As she had kept her vision clear in her mind, this did not work either!

Summary:

When we are vampirised we may become vampires ourselves to replenish our lost energy.

We remain in the realms of the vampires by living in a House of Horrors where all our energy goes into miserable lifestyle choices.

We can keep vampires at bay by shining the light of our awareness upon our relationships.

Summary of Tips:

Alter your habits, so that you focus on joyful living and not the House of Horrors.

Look for the good in everything and practice forgiving others and yourself.

Refuse to allow the vampire to "cross the threshold" through awareness.

Chapter 5

How to feel loved

Discover:
Why your Life's Purpose may be "To be yourself".
Life does not have to be a huge effort of will.
How to feel loved by connecting with everything.

Your Life's Purpose may be "To be yourself":

When we look to the outside of ourselves we begin to compare; whether people have achieved more or less than us according to our age, sex or situation, for example. From this we decide how we have failed or succeeded. However, when we look within we may realise that our lives are a journey of self-discovery and that simply learning to be oneself is the ultimate outcome.

What is growth?
Growing from a child into an adult is about discovering what is within. Many of us believe that we need to change on the inside, that we are not good enough as we are, that we must alter the way we think, act, react and behave. That, in fact, we are not acceptable as we are, that we need to change to become "good" or even "perfect".

Belief in perfection:
Do we believe in perfection? Those who claim, "nobody is perfect", are buying into the idea of perfection. This simple statement demonstrates how the individual's perception is that perfection is judged by what we see on the "outside". In other words, the way we behave, what we achieve, what we say and how others view us.

Perfection becomes a measure or a comparison between one person and another. We consider the quality of our work, or relationships to be a measure of perfection in ourselves. When something is not as we fantasise it should be, we call this failure or imperfection. When a partner or friends or colleagues behave in a way that does not conform to our fantasy of "how things should be" we judge them as imperfect, and may seek to "improve" them.

If you find yourself saying "nobody's perfect", then perhaps you need to challenge this thought and consider the notion that we are all perfect. We are all unique, and therefore comparison is irrelevant.

Comparisons:

To look at one flower and criticise it for having a different colour, shape or fragrance to another seems ridiculous. And yet we continually make comparisons between this one and that one, him and her, ourselves and others. These comparisons undermine the truth at our centre; that as unique individuals we can release the need to compare to others, and simply discover and rejoice in being ourselves.

By externalising perfection we create an impossible model to fulfil. In other words, when we try to live up to idealised expectations we find we will almost always fail (they are idealised, not real). To paraphrase the Zen Master on hearing two initiates arguing, "You are right, and you are also right".

To reject that we are perfection within ourselves is to fail to trust ourselves to achieve our potential. It means we are continually judging and rating ourselves against a yardstick that can only measure what is unachievable.

Letting go of "trying":

All the while that we hold onto the view that perfection can be measured, we are perpetually "trying to succeed". The problem with trying is that it implies failure. If I try to be perfect it has an integral "get out clause" - trying is all you will do; achieving does not go with this.

When we say, "I will try to succeed" we are automatically suggesting failure to ourselves. The message implicit is "I will go so far towards success, but am more confident in my failing to make the grain than in my ability to wholly succeed."

The promise to try:

When promising to try we are expecting that we will not succeed. A good example would be to reply to the request "please complete this task by the end of the day on Friday," with "I will try". This answer means "I will not"; the possible alternative is to say, "I will succeed", or " I can not complete the task by then, but I can complete it by ..."

Once we commit ourselves to trying, rather than achieving, we have already accepted that we may fail, and therefore failure becomes our only reality. We have no faith in success. Becoming angelic requires that you release the need to try and accept and trust the ability to succeed in being perfect.

What is perfection in humans?

When a baby is born we look on in awe and wonder and its beauty and perfection. What happens to change this perfect being into a doubting "trying but failing adult?"

Every single human being is totally unique. No two are identical, even twins who look similar, have different DNA, different characters. Therefore, we all bring with us our uniqueness. Who is to say what aspect of that should be judged to be good, or better, or worse than another?

What is our life's purpose?

The answer is simple, and yet challenging. Consider the notion that we are born into the world to be ourselves.

If this is true then our efforts to change ourselves in order to become perfect are wasted and ultimately doomed. If this is true then we need to find who we are and become happy and harmonised in being that person.

We need to trust ourselves and the process of life, and in doing so we can achieve our "perfection".

Imagine what life would be like if we did not have to change, but instead had only to allow ourselves to unfold. Our purpose will become apparent to us when we let go of the need to "discover it" - we allow the inner self to grow and reveal itself to us.

This requires shifting our focus to the authentic person within, and taking the spotlight off everything that is around and external to ourselves.

How should we judge good and evil?

When we are true to our authentic selves we are able to fully connect with the universe around us, without the need for comparison and competition. When we can value ourselves as part of this whole, we realise that to damage one is to damage the whole.

To attack an individual is like one cell of the body attacking another. Unless the system as a whole can overcome it, it will cause the demise of the body.

Therefore to judge and condemn others misses the point. We need to be looking at the truth within ourselves if we are to find it elsewhere. The Native American approach is an attempt to bring about a return to harmony, so that the most compelling action is the one that brings the whole community back to that sense of unity.

In judging others we are being egocentric, concerning ourselves with our own agenda, and not on the greater needs of the community as a whole. This is true within our relationships. That to judge a partner, for example, is to focus on the outside of ourselves, which implies that we are denying the inner self.

Before we begin to judge others we need to look within. Whenever we are presented with a situation in which we naturally desire to judge and condemn, we need to consider how this situation challenges our self perception, what is it about this situation that makes us feel compelled to judge? The answer can only be found within, as the subconscious or the Higher Self holds all the answers to our questions.

What is potential?

Potential is defined in the Oxford English Dictionary as "Capable of coming into being or action, usable resources, ability to do work by virtue of position, possibility or promise of development." The word itself is often used in relation to energy, such as with electrical impulses. The "Action Potential" within a brain cell is the ability to create an "electrical" impulse, which is the transmission of information and thinking.

When we consider our personal potential we may consider it to be our belief about our ability – our feeling that we may be capable of more. We may see potential as our ability to learn, an opportunity for us to improve, our future options.

Words that may help to encapsulate potential could include: likely, able, possible, capable, dormant, latent, implied, inherent, possibility. Potential is what we *don't know we can do - not* what we know we can do!

In my role as training consultant I have defined the potential of an individual as *the ability to understand that he or she has greater qualities within that can be drawn into the world.* Therefore, potential can be seen as an inner quest.

Fulfilment of potential involves these inner hidden qualities becoming available and a part of that individual's manner of interacting with his or her world.

Potential is a state of mind. In other words, it is an untapped reserve within an individual, and it only exists when we recognize that it may be there. If we do not accept or understand that our perception is the limiting factor we are locked in a paradox, whereby we will only see potential when we believe it has already been fulfilled.

Potential as latent energy:

I see potential as closely linked to energy, and I describe it as latent energy; that is, energy that is available if we know how to tap into it. We all have potential and therefore latent energy. This latent energy is available but currently unused, perhaps the individual does not know that he or she has the inner capability to develop.

Energy Vampirism and Potential:

Vampirism destroys our ability to recognise and tap into our latent energy or potential. When we lose sight of our own potential, when we do not recognise our inner abilities and fail to take on the inner quest, it is often because we have been sapped by a vampire.

This is never more obvious than at work. If you have a particularly dissatisfying job, you are very likely to be under the influence of a vampire. Those people who find their job a miserable and stressful aspect of their lives are probably suffering from an energy block, and this can be caused by the inability to tap into the latent energy of their potential. The end result is often Burn Out.

Life does not have to be a huge effort of will.

Sometimes "working at relationships" does not feel worth the effort. The struggle of managing other people in our lives can be demoralising and de-energising. When we realise that this outer struggle is actually an inner struggle, and that we are fighting ourselves, then we can discover that relationships can be easy.

Hanging onto life by the fingertips:

For many people life feels like a tremendous effort of will. As though we are climbing a mountain and just managing to hold on. The more tightly we grasp the rock face, the more insecure we feel. Sometimes we are holding on only by our fingertips, at other times we feel we have a foothold or two.

The weight we carry can be unbearably heavy, we may be carrying others as well as ourselves. It takes very little to dislodge us and then we are back to hanging from the mountain, waiting for the moment when we can hold on no more.

Attaching ourselves to anything or anyone means we are focusing our effort and will on external factors. By doing this we are denying that we can support ourselves. When life is hard work it demonstrates this: we are putting all our energy into maintaining an illusion, the illusion that we are in control of external events and people.

Control is one of the most elusive and yet desperately sought states of being. The more we attempt to control, the less we are able to achieve it. It is as though we are gripping a handful of sand, the more tightly we grasp the less we can hold onto it. Never was this more true than in relationships. The more we try to control our relationships the less we are able to do so, and the more dissatisfying they become.

Angelic Voices—Martin:

Martin had to give presentations as a regular part of his job, and yet he found the prospect terrifying. He spent the night before the presentation rehearsing and learning his "lines", and read and re-read his copious notes.

When he came to carry out the presentation he was always disappointed with the results, he came across as boring at best and muddled and lacking in knowledge at worst. He felt he compared poorly to his colleagues.

Martin sought the help of a coach, Mary, who he expected would give him tips on how to speak and his body language etc. In fact the coach did none of this. She asked Martin to run through the essentials of the presentation he was going to make to her informally, in particular, she wanted Martin to get across what he really wanted the audience to feel and what he wanted them to do.

Martin gave an impassioned talk, without the use of any notes, he alluded to some figures, but only gave rough estimates, because the message was the important part. Mary sat back and told Martin that he did not need any more help! Martin was amazed and a little cross. He complained that Mary had really not "done anything at all, and that he was not sure about paying her fee"! Mary smiled and told Martin that if he was clear on his intent and held the vision (knowing what he wanted to achieve) then all he would need to do was trust himself and work from the heart, from his passion. It suddenly dawned on Martin that he had actually made a presentation to Mary without any notes or visual aids. It also occurred to him that he had just made an exceptional and convincing presentation.

"Now," said Mary, "All you have to do is trust yourself and you can do the same thing every time!". Martin paid Mary and has recommended her to many of his colleagues, so that they can brush up on their skills!

Emotional Hypothermia:

The problem of a vampiric exchange of energy is that it is not nourishing. In order to feel good we need a constant inward flow of energy. As soon as the flow stops we feel insecure and vulnerable, we fear that we are not cared for, that our power over others has diminished. We do not feel loved, and that creates a vacuum within us.

This process is like the warm air of a weather system rising. Imagine the warm feeling of being loved by someone, and then imagine how it can dissipate quickly when they are no longer around to constantly validate us. When we need validation from another, we are exercising the vampire. The coldness of the vampire creeps in as the warmth of the feeling of love rises out of us.

Fig 5.1 **I am a Rock:**
In the song by Simon and Garfunkel "I am a Rock", the lyrics describe an individual who is determined to cut himself off from the pain of relationships.
The song sounds strong and brazen. "I have no need for friendship, friendship causes pain".
"Don't talk of love, Well I've heard the word before, its sleeping in my memory, I won't disturb the slumber of feelings that have died, If I never loved I never would have cried."
However, the last lines are:
"And a rock feels no pain, And an island never cries."
The song demonstrates that we can try to cut ourselves off from pain but end up being cut off from ourselves, and from the flow of love that is infinite in the universe. We prevent ourselves from being able to feel love.
The more we try to separate ourselves from the possibility of hurt the less we are open to the possibility of love. At this point we become more dependent than ever on vampiristic energy.

We feel empty inside and need to replenish ourselves, but the coldness numbs us to real feelings, rather than authentic feelings, we are confused by this emotional hypothermia, we see only what is outside ourselves. We see love as existing outside. External love is seen as a means of becoming warm and whole, and yet it also feels unobtainable. At these moments we can feel desperate. Where is the love? Why am I so unlovable? Why do I feel like this? These thoughts rush around our heads, and we greedily look for a quick fix; "Who can make me feel better?".

Once we have fed off another again, the process repeats, the feeling will always subside because it is not sustainable. Once the energy is used, it must be replaced, and the vampire within us seeks to replace it by the best means it knows, by feeding off someone else.

Feelings of Desperation:

Many of us go through feelings of desperation at some point in our lives. These feelings are extreme versions of the emotional hypothermia we can experience and they need to be understood in order to prevent them from becoming life threatening.

Sadly, there are times when people feel they cannot continue to live without this "external" love. Others may become deeply depressed by the anxiety that is created when they doubt that they may be able to feel loved again.

When this happens in our lives, we need to remember that it is only the effect of having a supply of love cut off, either temporarily or permanently, but this does not mean that we cannot find the feeling of being loved again.

| Fig 5.2 **Recognising Emotional Hypothermia and Energy Self Regulation:** ||
Emotional Hypothermia:	**Maintaining Energy Self Regulation:**
Feeling cold, emotions numbed.	Open to feelings, even those that cause pain: grief, sadness, anger, fear etc.
Vulnerability.	Knowing that security is found within.
Fear—do not understand why one feels like this.	Awareness of one's feelings, realisation that any fear may be due to hypothermia and that this is within one's control.
Feeling out of control.	Able to take proactive steps.
Desperation—feeling alone.	Ability to connect to the universe (or God depending upon your beliefs). Able to enjoy one's own company in the empty moments.

For some, rediscovering love can be a slow process, but this is not always the case, and the most important energiser that we can draw upon is hope.

The numb and empty feeling that can create emotional hypothermia may be caused when we lose a loved one, such as on death or the end of a relationship. However, other events can cause similar feelings, such as loss of a job, a friendship ending, being separated from people that are important to us.

The more able we are to connect to the universal energy flow, the better we can cope with the ebb and flow of our lives; we feel loved when we connect with everything,

 Angelic Voices—Ralph (Overcoming Emotional Hypothermia):
I was alone in my hotel room, having been away from home for only a week, when I suddenly felt a terrible feeling in the pit of my stomach, almost like I had been punched, and at the same time a diabolical sense of loneliness and despair crept over me.

I wanted to cry, but no tears came. I stood for an hour looking out of the window at the car park. I felt numb, and at that moment I even contemplated ending it all. This was extraordinary and out of character for me. I could not understand where the feelings had come from.

I spoke to my wife later that day and felt a little better, but I was pleased that I would be going home soon.

Once I had realised I was suffering from emotional hypothermia I knew what steps to take. First of all, I knew I had to warm up, so I took this literally and had a warm bath, then wrapped up in some comfortable clothes and had a cup of tea. Then I made a list of all the wonderful things that I had in my life, strangely I shed a couple of tears, but felt better, remembering how much I love my family.

I realised that the work I was doing was not satisfying me, but that I did not have to allow it to drain my energy. I spent some time thinking about how I could value myself. This created an immediate change in my mood, and I became able to enjoy the moments of peace I had with myself.

Energy Self Regulation:

The ideal state is one where we are energy "self regulating" this means "staying the same ". It is usually used to refer to animals that are able to regulate their internal functions such as their own temperature, in other words they are able to maintain a constant internal temperature. We call these kinds of animals warm blooded.

Self-Regulating responses are demonstrated by mammals, including humans, which have a consistent body temperature, and use internal means to regulate this. For example, when we are cold we shiver to warm ourselves, we go white because our blood is redirected into the body to prevent loss of heat through the skin, and we have a layer of subcutaneous fat to provide insulation.

When we are warm we cool down by sweating, we go red because the blood comes closer to the surface of our skin in order to lose heat more quickly etc.

Energy Self Regulation is similar. It is the means by which we can retain a regularised energy flow, so that we do not end up with a vacuum. Instead, we ensure that we lose any excess heat and yet retain enough to keep us emotionally warm and snug.

Overcoming Emotional Hypothermia:

Emotional hypothermia, a feeling of desperation, can set in very quickly, as can be seen in the Case Study "Ralph". In order to overcome emotional hypothermia we need to discover how to awaken the inner angel, and this is covered in greater detail in Part 2.

However, here are some quick fixes:

Make sure you feel physically warm and take any measures that will make you feel cosy, these may be to have a warm bath, to wrap up in comfortable clothes, to have a cup or tea.

Avoid drinking alcohol—imagine the effects on hypothermia, if you drink alcohol you may immediately warm up, but you will lose heat again very quickly. Similarly, with emotional hypothermia the effects of alcohol may be to

Fig 5.3 **Emotional Holy Hot Water Bottles**	
Cold thoughts are those that relate to vampiristic behaviours:	**Warm thoughts activate the angels inside:**
Self criticism	Self acceptance/ Self Love
Criticism of others	Acceptance of others
Blame	Taking responsibility for one's feelings and behaviour
Failing to take responsibility for oneself—feeling the world is "unfair".	Being self sufficient, not expecting energy fixes, but being prepared to be proactive in solving problems of energy deficiency
Non authentic emotions, for example, failing to accept fear, and turning it into anger against someone else.	Authentic feelings—experiencing ones emotions as they are without trying to rationalise them.

feel better immediately, but to feel much worse when it has worn off.

Get into daylight—this can be literal, by taking a walk outside, or metaphorical, by shining light on your thoughts and activating awareness of what is happening. By noticing that you are simply suffering from emotional hypothermia you can quickly arrest the process by understanding that it is not an authentic feeling, but a reaction to the events around you.

Count your blessings and make a list of the things that support you in life.

Think about all the aspects of yourself that you love or like.

Douse yourself with "Holy Water" in order to maintain "pure thoughts". In other words, do not criticise yourself, or anyone else, at all. If you find criticism creeping in, banish it. Focus on good and supportive thoughts only.

Get into some authentic feelings. This will usually happen when you have carried out the above. In other words, allow yourself to feel the real feelings you have about the situation. The difficulty is that you may not be able to rationalise them, or relate them to the situation. This often happens when people feel like crying "for no reason". When we try to bring "reason" into the emotion we are cutting ourselves off from authentic feeling and are creating an unreal stunted emotional outburst. Frequently, but not always, this is demonstrated by anger.

Why is control over another dissatisfying?

How much control over another will make us feel good? The answer is that there can never be enough, once we have exerted control and succeeded we do not stop and say, "Thank you, that is all I require". On the contrary, maintaining control is a full time occupation; a perpetual and exhausting process, because control is not love. This is why we are inevitably dissatisfied by relationships that we seek to control.

Love is the only commodity that can satisfy in any measure. Unconditional love is open ended both in being given and received. Conditional love is not love at all; it is approval. Love can only truly be love when it is unconditional.

Control is dissatisfying because we cannot define what is enough control and so there can never be enough.

How to feel loved by connecting with everything.

Energy is love. And love is the connection between the universe and us. When we are able to connect in a loving way to everything, work, home, family, friends, environment, then we energise these connections. As every connection is energised we feel completely loved and we no longer need to cling to attachments.

Love and energy may be one and the same:

If we are to understand the vampire's thirst for energy, we need to understand what we mean by energy and from where we draw it. We all have the ability to tap into an inexhaustible supply of energy. We know this is true, although we often deny it, because we are able to feel energised by people, events and things. Think about a time when you felt physically exhausted, and yet, at the prospect of doing something enjoyable you were suddenly full of energy!

Scientists may describe the universe as being comprised of energy. When contemplating the universe from a spiritual perspective we may describe it as being love. These two opinions may seem at odds with each other, but in effect they may be they identifying the same phenomenon, but using a different yardstick. This is because we can view love and energy to be one and the same. The physicist wants to quantify and measure, and yet, there is one thing even a scientist will agree is an absolute truth to man and womankind and yet it cannot be measured or seen, and its presence is only known when it is felt: love.

Love energises us when we receive it unconditionally from people for whom we care. Love energises us when we experience beauty. The satisfaction of endeavour or achievement can fill us with good feelings about ourselves, when we feel self-respect, self-esteem and self-approval, inner love is energising us.

Energy can be seen at work in every aspect of our lives, in our jobs, with our friends, colleagues, parents, children and other family members and in the day to day dealings we have with people from as diverse situations as shopping to going to the doctor.

How energy can be seen in our lives:

There are many ways of defining energy, but it is best understood as the power of love. Energy exists as part of the universe. It flows through all of creation, and you are connected to the wholeness of the universe through this flow.

It is available for all, just as love is available for all, and yet some of us have difficulty in gaining access to it.

Scientifically energy in the body is the result of a conversion of carbohydrates and proteins in our diet. So it is not surprising that we often find ourselves comfort eating to compensate for energy loss through vampirism. However, the energy to which I refer is not a direct result of this chemical reaction.

This energy is the life force that motivates and drives us, is our passion and, when latent, our potential. This is the energy that we can draw upon at will, that can make changes in our lives through contemplation and thought and can fill others and ourselves with sensations of peace and well being.

This is the energy that creates our health, enabling us to overcome any difficulties or ailments with our inner resolve and belief. This energy can make us feel enthusiastic and cogent. It can take us into dangerous and frightening situations and out the other side unharmed. It is the energy that, with the odds against us, helps us to pass that examination, make that speech, tell the truth to our parents, protect and defend our children or friends, passionately stand up for our belief in what is right.

When we see this energy at work it is an awesome sight. People who are able to draw energy into themselves seem to glow with it. Energy is an attractive force; we naturally tend to move towards a source of energy, as we would naturally seek to feed. Health guru and "red-nosed doctor" Patch Adams advocates following your passion in life, and yet provides a warning that passionate people are attractive to those who would sap their energy.

Where our energy comes from:

When we are born we are attached to our mothers by the umbilical cord. Through this cord we receive all the goodness from our mother. The blood of our mother feeds us with nutrients, oxygen and energy. This attachment is so strong that after parturition, when the cord is cut, we feel as though it is still there.

Like an amputee continues to feel the limb that has been removed, we continue to sense the umbilical and rely on it as a newborn.

When we are born our mother is our universe, we are "egocentric", believing that we are at the centre of this universe. We derive all our energy from our mother and those who freely connect to us, those who love us.

The process of growing and developing allows us the opportunity to release this attachment and find our way to being self supporting. We do this by finding all our energy needs are provided for in the universe.

The universe is our ultimate source of energy. In order to develop into fully fledged independent beings we must detach from others and source our energy from the universe.

Learning to be human means learning to sever attachments, just as the umbilical was cut, and in so doing find that we are supported wholly.

The divine paradox is this: when we have no attachments we are ultimately supported, and fully connected. When we grasp hold of any available strand hoping it will carry our weight, we are at the greatest risk because we invest our energy in the fear that we might fall.

Trust as the basis for Angelic Living:

Coach, counsellor and guru, Chuck Spezanno defines trust as "wherever you choose to invest the power of your mind". This definition perfectly integrates with Angelic Living because it first requires that you have trust in yourself.

What do you trust?

Look at your life to determine in what you place your trust. Do you trust yourself to be successful? To have abundance? To be popular? Or do you trust yourself to fail? To be in debt? To have no friends?

Trust is a key component in relationships. However, it is often placed externally. In other words, we put our trust where we cannot control it—with someone else. By doing this we create expectations that will almost always be dashed, as our partner, friend or colleague will be unlikely to fulfil them. It is difficult enough to live up one's own expectations without trying to live up to those of another.

Trust is the opposite of "hanging onto life by the fingertips". When we trust we discover the paradoxical truth, we do not need to hold on, as the universe holds onto us when we trust. How can this be? The answer is to look at the way the universe works. The sun does not need to be held up in the sky, the earth revolves around the sun and the entire universe follows its pathway, regardless of our desires or will. We accept that there is enough oxygen to breathe; we accept that our bodies will continue to keep us alive, our heart beating and our lungs respiring.

To worry or concern ourselves about this would be to expend energy futilely. We know that to worry about how long we will live will not actually extend our lives; on the contrary. All this requires our trust.

If we are to succeed in allowing the universe to support us, we have to let go! If we are to allow our relationships to support us, we must let go of the attachment and begin to energise the connections.

Why will the universe be supportive?

The universe supports us because we are the universe. There is no separation between each of us and the universe as a whole.

This means that we are all connected, but that we may not energise these connections. When we do we experience love.

When we are able to work with this concept of unity and move out of separation, we can effectively source our energy from the universe. In other words, when we criticise another, we are really criticising ourselves.

Energising Connections:

Every time we connect we are experiencing love, although we may not realise it; for example, when we stand and look at a beautiful view and feel moved, or when we meet someone with whom we feel we have an affinity, or when we show compassion.

We can feel love when we demonstrate it. This is what we mean by connecting with everything in a loving way. For example, how often do we feel anger with inanimate objects? Computers are a great example of this. We can shout abuse at them swear and curse them. When we do this we are cutting off connections, because the reality is, we are attacking ourselves. In this situation we feel unloved and unlovable, and will often be aggressive towards the people who wish to come to our aid.

Our partners may feel unloved because they perceive and feel the anger that we are demonstrating and its fallout makes them feel personally attacked.

If we can connect with everything, even inanimate objects, in a loving way, we will energise the connections between our world and ourselves. And the more connections we energise the more love *we feel.*

The extraordinary thing about this is that when we feel loved we become satisfied with our lives, we have what we need, and yet it is not being "given" by someone else. It is found within ourselves.

How to connect and energise:

From the moment you begin the day think kindly upon everything with which you come into contact; appreciate everything deeply.

Appreciate the beauty and/or usefulness of inanimate objects, see the loveliness of nature, feel the freshness of the air. Look upon every face you see, the young and the old, and see the beauty. Appreciate every person you come into contact with, feel kindly towards everyone, even the person who cuts you up at the roundabout when you are driving to work; perhaps he has had a difficult morning? Perhaps he made a simple error? Let go of the anger, resentment and irritation, and instead think kindly.

Spend a day lovingly connecting with everything, and see the difference it makes. You will feel happy, secure, relaxed and peaceful. In other words, you will feel loved, as though there is a glow of love around you, and you are wallowing right in the middle of it. You will not feel alone, because you will feel and be a part of everything.

When you have experienced this, you will realise that to find love is easy, and that love, that infinite resource, will steadily seek you out.

***

Fig 5.4 : Letting Go—Money

Money probably causes more problems in relationships than anything else. When we worry about our debts it prevents us from taking positive action, and we become embroiled in a belief in scarcity.

We must connect lovingly with money too, and to do this we must also realise that money is only a form of energy, it is a means of exchanging one thing for another. When we release the fear of having too little and connect lovingly with money we attract stability and abundance to us.

When we try too hard to make money we are "hanging on by the fingertips" and finance becomes a struggle. Trust is the answer.

The universal laws will support you when you trust them.

***

Summary:

You were born perfect, and you may only need to use this lifetime to rediscover that perfection.

When we let go and allow ourselves to trust that everything will work as we intend, the universe supports us. Even when things do not go as planned, we must continue to trust because the outcome of trust will always serve us in the end.

You can feel loved by connecting with everything in a loving way. Once you do this, unstoppable and infinite love will pour into your life.

Summary of Tips:

Stop trying. Instead either make a promise you can succeed in achieving, or let go of the promise. Do not set yourself up for failure by attempting to do or to be more than is possible for you.

Let go of perfection. Accept that whatever happens will be perfect, even if you have to search for the reasons why it is perfect.

Practice trusting by beginning each day with a simple affirmation: "I trust that I will be supported by the universe in all that I do."

Connect lovingly with everything. This includes inanimate objects, feel loving thoughts about everything you do and everyone you meet. *Especially* those people who criticise you and the computer when it goes wrong! Your loving thoughts will create a transformation in your energy and will create magical changes in your life. Love will seek you out.

The Guilt Vampire

Chapter 6

The Process of Awakening

Discover:
That if you see a vampire, you are a vampire.
How to awaken angels in your life and relationships.
How to use the ACT approach to make changes in your life

If you see a vampire, you are a vampire.

The vampire is invisible in the mirror. We cannot see ourselves as vampires, we delude ourselves that they are "out there" when really they are within.

Hold up a mirror:

Vampires fear mirrors because, as it is well documented in many stories and films, they cannot see themselves in the glass. In the case study below we can see how victims can become invisible, as they transform into the vampire.

The process of becoming invisible is due to a loss of identity. When we search for who we are we fail to see ourselves as whole people, our personality appears to fragment, and we see only the component parts. When we see our faces we see a collection of features and not the whole person.

This is frequently experienced when we have been victims of vampirism for some time. Our loss of identity extends to the way we view ourselves, even as far as what we actually perceive when we see ourselves in the mirror.

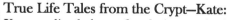 ### True Life Tales from the Crypt—Kate:

Kate realised that, after being sucked of life force, she could no longer see herself in the mirror – she no longer recognised the translucent face.

Kate had been the victim of vampirism at work; she had experienced a Charismatic boss who had slowly bled her of ideas and enthusiasm and whenever she felt she was making progress, he would knock her back with criticism that she could not counter. And yet, the criticism was almost impossible to rectify; she was often placed in a Catch 22 position, whereby she would be expected to deliver results, and yet would be starved of the resources to do so. Her creative efforts to circumvent this would give her an immediate boost in the eyes of her boss, who would heap unrealistic expectations upon her which would result in a rapid decline when he was ultimately dissatisfied.

Those around her noticed the effect on Kate. She seemed to be a different person; her personality changed. It was difficult to define in exactly what ways, but she had lost her enthusiasm and positivism, there was a cynical undercurrent to her, and, unsurprisingly, her energy was low. She seemed perpetually tired and not the fun and energetic person she had once been.

It was a moment of truth for her when she realised that the person she was looking at in the mirror did not resemble herself at all. It was this that alerted her to her change. She was now looking into the face of the beast; she was now the vampire.

Continually check on your own behaviour. Have you allowed your vampire to rise from the grave? Can you awaken your angel instead?

Invisible Children:
We may be creating invisible children or may have been an invisible child. When we speak about a child in his earshot, but as though he is not there, we treat him as if he is invisible. After a while the child responds to this by behaving as if he is invisible.

This trait can occur in adulthood, both the "parent" behaviour, speaking about someone as if they are not there, and the "child" response" to behave as if invisible.

 ### Angelic Voices — Cassie:
Cassie was a young mother who was determined to bring up her child with the love and affection, attention and encouragement that she lacked as a child. Her son Paul was an active and dominant child, and at two years old, the problem for Cassie was in knowing how to control Paul's curiosity. He was so bright and interested that he was "into everything" and considered "a little monster" at the Play group she visited.

Cassie was only too well aware of the opinion of other people, and would discuss the problems she had with Paul. She was always willing to learn.

On one occasion Cassie was visiting the Playgroup head teacher with Paul, who insisted on misbehaving and refused to listen to Cassie when she told him to stop fiddling with the computer or the filing cabinet drawers. After telling Paul to stop Cassie turned to the Playgroup teacher, Marion, and said, "This is the problem I have with him, he never listens to me or does what I tell him, I don't know what to do about it".

Marion noticed that Cassie maintained the same tone of voice throughout and that, when it suited him, Paul seemed to ignore not only Cassie's instructions but her whole existence.

This gave Marion an insight; if Cassie treated Paul as if he could not understand or hear her when she was talking about him to others, perhaps he felt invisible, and so, if he was invisible, so was Cassie. Paul was using the same behaviours with Cassie as she used with him. He ignored her because he felt invisible.

Marion advised Cassie always to speak to Paul, and involve him in any conversations when he is present, never to assume he would not understand anything she said, and reward him when he became visible. Most importantly, Cassie needed to become visible again too. Marion advised her, whenever she spoke to Paul, to go right up to him and make sure he made eye contact with her.

Cassie found this advice quite difficult to carry out initially, but quickly she realised that they were communicating with each other; sometimes the communication was angry and Paul would have a tantrum, but this soon calmed down and their relationship moved onto a new level and both became much more satisfied. Cassie admitted that it took a great deal more work to love Paul this way, but, equally, it was a great deal more rewarding for them both. Paul became happier at Playgroup and much easier to manage.

The Danger in Looking for Vampires:

If we start looking for vampires, we will find them. Once we become aware of these creatures of the night it is difficult not to see them everywhere. They will begin to crawl out of the woodwork of every relationship we have, they will claw and beckon, they will drain and destroy. Just as in Stephen King's novel "Salem's Lot", the Vampire Slayers role appears to be a never-ending roller coaster ride of staking vampires. It becomes our life's work. Instead we must realise that the only vampire we can slay is the one within ourselves. We need to realise that it is we who reside in the dark, and therefore, we must find our own way back into the light.

The spectrum of vampire behaviours:

Most of us have the full range of vampire behaviours at our fingertips. Each and every one of the different vampire archetypes lives within us, and may be looking for an opportunity to rise and dominate us.

What vampires are you seeing?

It is easy to discover which inner vampires are haunting your subconscious. You simply look at the vampires that are affecting your life. These are the ones that you need to deal with. For example, if you have a Charismatic Vampire in your life, you need to look within at your inner Charismatic Vampire, it is almost certain to be on the prowl.

If you are being vampirised by a Needy Vampire, watch out! You are probably bringing your Needy Vampire into the world of the living for a feast. The same is true for each of the others.

Once we become aware of vampires we may begin to see them wherever we go. This does not mean that the world is full of the undead. Every vampire you see is like a reflection of the vampire within you, and our vampire cannot see itself in the mirror. Once we become aware we can look within and neutralise our own vampire in order to rid ourselves of the vampires in our lives.

What is your role in the machinations of vampires?

Even if you feel you do not have a role in the games of vampires, you must be in some way involved with them. It takes courage to admit that even listening to rumours creates a response somewhere.

In the black comedy film "Dance of the Vampires—Pardon me, but your teeth are in my neck", starring Sharon Tate and Roman Polanski, the three vampire hunters accidentally find themselves at the Vampires' Ball, amongst hundreds of dancing vampires. They decide that the best way to avoid capture is to become involved with the ball, and all three join in Minuet.

After a while they are enjoying themselves so much that they more or less forget with whom they are dancing; that is, until they simultaneously turn and find themselves, and the whole room of vampires, staring into the wall length mirror. They are the only three people reflected. Their joyful expressions fall as they realise they are no longer dancing partners, but have become the hors d'oeuvres

The lesson is simple. You cannot dance with vampires without getting bitten.

The Needy Vampire

How to awaken angels in your life and relationships.

When we awaken the inner angels, miraculously, we discover that there are angels surrounding us, and that we were not previously aware of how to see them.

Looking for angels:

Now we have spent some time considering the inner vampires, we can begin the search for the inner angel.

Angelic behaviour is self-supporting, when we use the inner angel we discover that we have all the support from the universe that we need. We do not feel insecure or alone, we do not suffer from Emotional Hypothermia, and we feel energised and happy within ourselves.

We all have an inner angel. Just as we can all choose to let the vampire rise, we can equally choose to awaken the angel. When we do so, we are able to:

- Awaken Joy—Feel joy in all aspects of our lives now
- Awaken Passion—Allow our wounds to heal and discover our power
- Awaken Freedom—Feel free of our need for others
- Awaken Courage—Let ourselves shine
- Awaken Truth—Be able to satisfy our needs
- Awaken Love—Make love a reality in our lives

In order to do this we need to take a simple step by step approach. As we go through each step we discover how the angel is personified within us.

When we learn how angels can be awakened within ourselves, we discover that our moments of deepest loneliness are in fact the moments when we are closest to our true inner self, that at these times we can feel secure and happy in our knowledge of ourselves. We become our own companion.

By Awakening Angels we move from a somnambulistic, or sleep walking, state to wakefulness. We begin to see life as it really is, rather than under a veil of judgement, comparison and separation from the whole.

When we "let go" of our need for attachment to people and our need to feel loved and approved of, we find we are supported by life and realise that we cannot feel secure when we are frantically grappling for a finger hold

In this part of the book you will be able to take practical steps towards awakening the angel in your relationships. In order to do this you need first to awaken the angel in yourself, and then be able to seek it out in others. This requires a new approach to everything you do.

Each step is easy in theory, but it takes application and determination to ensure you keep going and do not give up.

How to use the ACT approach to make changes in your life.

In the second part of this book, each chapter has a simple and effective method of enabling change; it is know as ACT

ACT is a mnemonic that helps you to remember the three key stages in making changes in your life that will help you to awaken angels in your relationships, and stands for:

Action primer
Change thinking
Transform habits

Action Primer:

Before can make changes to your life, you need to carry out the essential preparation. If not, you will find that you quickly lose momentum and go back to old ways.

The Action Primer is a way of shaking the foundations. In other words, you begin gently to unravel what your life is like right now so that you can prime yourself for making real and lasting changes.

When we make changes in our lives we need to consider how these can be part of the "big picture". The best way to understand this is to imagine a mosaic. When standing up close it appears to be fragmented, made up of individual pieces. However, when you stand back the overall picture can be seen, and the small fragmented parts disappear.

Likewise, when working with changes you need to be able to work with the individual pieces, whilst simultaneously seeing how they fit into the whole picture. You need to take a broad view of your life, as well as looking at the detail.

Where the small parts are not fitting harmoniously into the whole we must reassess and re-carve them. If we do not, they will quickly be dislodged and we return to old patterns that fit better, even if they are unproductive.

Change Thinking:

Action always follows thought. So, if you want to change the way you act, you need to change the thought processes that initiate the action.

This is where you make actual changes to the way you work, by changing the way you think. Now we are looking for action, as opposed to preparation.

At the end of each chapter in part 2 you will find that there are some "Change

Thinking" Assignments. These may be:

Walking Mantra -this is a simple affirmation that you may choose to say to yourself at any moment during the day, or when you feel it would be supportive to do so. The walking mantra is individual to you; so you do not need to use one of the suggestions, but they are powerful and effective, so make sure you have at least one on the go at any one time.

Thought Shifting Exercises - these may simply be ideas to contemplate. They may be things to notice. Through becoming more aware you will automatically de-select behaviours that undermine you, and will discover that more angelic solutions will begin to filter through.

Transform Habits:

The third stage in changing our life is to transform our habits. It is difficult to make changes in our lives at the best of times, because our habits take over, and before we realise it, we have "reverted to type", and are back doing things in the old ways, even though these ways may not be serving us.

You will be provided with tips and pointers for changing the old habits you have for new, rewarding ones, as you go through the book. I recommend that you try to implement just one or two at a time, and when that is established, then try to implement the next.

In this way you can make big changes by taking small steps.

Here are some tips:

When you have managed to make a small change, no matter how tiny, please celebrate and congratulate yourself. Even if it is just when you notice that you are being a vampire, or choose not to use vampire behaviours.

Most importantly, catch yourself when you are "getting it right". That way you can build on the positives.

By building upon these small changes you can shape your future, because your future is the sum of everything you think, do and say right now. If you do not reward yourself you will immediately slip back into pain and darkness.

Awakening involves being in the light. When we wake up in the morning the light can hurt our eyes, and we may want to snuggle back down under the covers. However, we know that if we are to get anything done, we have to get up and welcome the new day. After we have stretched and yawned we can look out the window into the morning light and enjoy the vibrancy of all the colours, the light playing on the cars and trees. We can feel energised and ready for action.

If we jump up too quickly and act before we are truly awake we can feel tired and muddled all day, and would ideally slip right back into bed at any opportunity. But if we give ourselves time to awaken, and enjoy the process, we can find the whole day is more productive and enjoyable.

This is true for awakening your angel. It may be painful to begin with, but when your angel is fully awake and functioning, you will be energised and excited by life. Allow your inner angel to guide you, do not fight against it, or fail to trust it: when we do this we are clinging on, and life is more difficult; when we relax and go with the flow we allow the angel within us all to grow and shine.

Finally, it is worth remembering this story– Footsteps:

A man arrived in the next world; he was greeted by his angel, and looked back at the life he had left.

He could see his life was like a map, and he could follow his progress by spotting the footprints that marked the steps he had taken. As he looked carefully he noticed that sometimes there were two sets of prints and sometimes there was only one. This perturbed him, so he spoke to his angel and asked it, "Why are there sometimes two sets of prints on my life's pathway?"

His angel, who had been noticing his perplexity, explained, "There are two sets of footprints because I was travelling beside you".

The man was greatly comforted by this, and looked more closely still at his map. He noticed that when the terrain was easy and flat there were two sets of footprints, but when the terrain was rocky and treacherously steep, there was only one set.

Again the man became perplexed and a little angry. "Why did you desert me in times of greatest need?" He asked his angel, feeling as though he had been struggling alone through the difficult patches of his life.

His angel replied, "I did not desert you".

"Then why are there only one set of prints when my need was greatest?" He cried.

The angel looked at him kindly, "That was because when times were easy I walked beside you, but when things were tough, I carried you".

(This story was adapted from one known as "Footsteps" and that I read in the Bolney Village Parish Magazine, I do not know the original author).

Chapter 7

Step 1- Awakening the Angel of Joy

Discover:
How to antidote the Corrupter Vampire
How to bring joy into your life now

How to antidote the Corrupter Vampire

Every moment of my life is precious. I live each precious moment in joy.

The Sunshine of Joy

The corrupter will seek power over others to fulfil its own ends with no compassion or care. The House of Horrors is represented by the Corrupter Vampire.

The Sunshine of Joy is the direct opposite of the House of Horrors. Here we feel loved and supported by our friends and family, we are full of energy, we notice that the world is awash with beauty and we take time to appreciate it. We find our children a joy to us, they stop being irritants, and they seem to behave better. Life appears to be easier, and even when times are hard, they do not seem to be so bad, as we are blessed with so much love and beauty.

How do we antidote the Corrupter Vampire within?

The Corrupter cannot survive in the light. When we throw the light of the Sunshine of Joy upon it, it shrivels up and dies. This means we need to exercise a childlike belief and trust in the Sunshine of Joy. Every time doubt creeps into your mind, every time you decide to moan about something that you saw on the TV and every time you choose blame rather than compassion you unleash the Corrupter.

The Corrupter will turn to dust in the daylight, so keep out of the shadows and allow the Angel of Joy to lift your spirits.

Using Daylight to turn the Vampire to Dust:

Daylight is a metaphor for the conscious mind, and the dark for the unconscious. We can 'turn the vampire to dust' by activating awareness. This is a simple yet powerful method for driving out our own vampire and banishing the vampire of others.

It is only when we become aware of our vampiric behaviour that we can change it. We need to look into the mirror and see what is real, we need to shine the light of our consciousness upon our behaviour and recognise what we really are or what we may be becoming.

Vampires do not cast a shadow:

Remember that vampires don't cast a shadow. If someone seems perfect, with no visible faults, you may be activating their vampire for them.

Are you trying to achieve perfection? Or can you accept yourself as you are? We can see this clearly demonstrated in ourselves when we only see "blame" on the outside and not from within. For example, when we have an argument with a loved one, we may spend a lot of time pointing the finger at what he or she is doing or has done that is wrong; how he or she created the disagreement by unreasonable behaviour, anger, disinterest etc.

All the time that we are doing this, we are failing to take responsibility for the situation; we feel vindicated because we have been "perfect" and it is his or her fault.

By noticing this we may be able to neutralise the vampire by taking time out to appreciate our own contribution to any disharmony. We need to remember that we must bear responsibility for communication breakdown, and that until we banish our vampire we will not be able to re-establish a positive means of connecting with another person.

How to bring Joy into your life now:

Things change when we allow the sunshine of joy of illuminate our world.

The Angel of Joy:

When we awaken the Angel of Joy we begin to see a shift in the way our lives work. The Angel of Joy cannot be seen as a specific character but more as a process. It is best understood by imagining the atmosphere just before an angel enters the room.

When people have reported "angelic experiences" they often describe a "floating feeling of warmth, love and peace." This is the sensation of the Angel of Joy. When we communicate directly from the heart we know we are in touch with the Angel of Joy that exists within each of us, and which is reaching out, because the force becomes stronger every time it connects with another heart.

Living in the Now:

The Angel of Joy represents the ability to live in the Now moment. In other words, to come to each moment as though it were completely fresh and new, untainted by the last moment and unaffected by the next one.

As you go through the different aspects of the Angel of Joy you will see that they underline this simple premise; to be happy in this moment is to be happy forever.

What is the Sunshine of Joy?

When we are immersed in Pain it is difficult to imagine that there is another way of being, but there is, and it is right here. The Sunshine of Joy exists in the here and now, and yet it may seem elusive, almost as though it is a parallel universe, and in a sense it is. In order to get into this "other world" we have to make a leap. You could call it a leap of faith.

Other worlds:

We can live in another world. But if we are to do this we need to be able to make a grand leap. In "The Magician's Nephew", the first book in The Lion, The Witch and The Wardrobe series, C.S. Lewis describes "The Wood between the Worlds". In this wood there are numerous small pools, and one enters the wood through one of the pools and leaves in the same way. However, if you choose to jump into one of the other pools you can enter another world, perhaps one that is dying or one that is just born.

By jumping into the pool you can be transported to another reality. But in order to jump we need to first let go of our belief in the House of Horrors. This is a jump into the abyss, and it is a leap of faith. When we take this leap we are rewarded by the discovery that we are being supported by life, and that no alteration to our lives is going to be threatening to us when we accept it.

Exercise: Count your blessings

Whatever the event, we can choose how we respond to it. Why waste energy being depressed, when we can count our blessings and feel the joy of being alive.

Let us weigh up what really matters in life; for most of us it is love. We can feel love for people, memories and animals, possessions that have beauty or attachment. However, the most real thing about this is the feeling.

Objects decay, people live and then pass on. Memories can become cloudy. Love is real forever. It lives beyond the grave. Those in poverty, the lonely, and the abused can feel it. Love is the greatest of all truths.

Remember every instance of love you have experienced, in whatever form it may have been. Whether it was for another human, a parent, sibling, friend or lover, or even a beloved pet.

"Count up" every loving experience you can recall. Note every good thing that you have in your life; a comfortable bed to sleep in, a good meal, children, friends, community. Once you have been through a list of these it is difficult not to feel a little better and more closely aligned to the Sunshine of Joy.

Fig 7.1 **Tips for Rediscovering the Joy Paradigm:**

- Express love frequently—show your love with contact
- Laugh when things go wrong—getting upset will not make them right again!
- Enjoy learning experiences, seek them out all the time.
- Make everyday a day when you learn something new
- Express yourself
- Do not judge the way others express themselves
- Find joy in the routine tasks

Rediscovering the Sunshine of Joy:

Hopefully, there is a place in your past or present where you were able to live within the Sunshine of Joy. As children, when our home life is secure and happy, we know joy. A perfect example of the Sunshine of Joy living is the pre-school children's television programme "Tellytubbies ".

In this world, the Tellytubbies "love each other very much" and frequently confirm this with "big hugs". When something "goes wrong" the Tellytubbies laugh, because, nothing actually goes wrong, it is all just an experience from which they will learn something new. Tellytubbies enjoy discovering more about life. They express themselves in the way that they feel comfortable and happy without judging each other. They find joy and excitement in everything they do, even the routine things. When you can live like a Tellytubby you too can live within the Sunshine of Joy!

Angelic Energisers: Tapping into a source of energy

How often have you felt exhausted after a long day at work, only to find your energy returns as soon as the prospect of something pleasurable comes to mind? This is evidence that energy is available to us, if we know how to tap into it. We can tap into energy when we recognise those things that fill us with a feeling of peace and contentment, in other words, with love.

The first step to tapping into universal energy is to find opportunities to experience Beauty and Companionship. This provides you with a means of drawing energy into yourself. Inner energy comes from self-esteem and therefore the second step is to find your inner value as a part of this beauty. When you can tap into this freely available energy you will find yourself reconnecting to joy.

Beauty:

When we appreciate beauty we enable ourselves to connect with universal love, or energy. We notice that we feel differently. We often notice this as a physical sensation as well as an emotional one. Our interpretation of beauty is individual, but for it to be energising it must be pure and never salacious. A beautiful woman may be inspiring, but only if the beauty is appreciated for its own sake and not for our own hidden agenda of self-satisfaction. For this reason, the beauty of nature, art and music is most able to inspire natural energy.

Exercise: Experiencing Beauty

The following exercise will help you to recognize when you are tapping into and being energised by the infinite pool of love from the universe.

Consider the most beautiful object or place you have ever seen. If possible, go to that place, or find a photograph to look at. Imagine you are there and seeing this for the first time all over again.

Imagine the most beautiful piece of music you have ever heard. Play the music if you have it and sit with your eyes closed, listening.

Find a favourite spot outside in nature, somewhere quiet and undisturbed if possible, and go and sit there. Drink in the beauty of the landscape around you, feel the breeze on your face and in your hair. Listen for sounds of birds or animals scuffling in the undergrowth.

In each case seek out the absolute beauty of the situation. Look for every small piece of evidence of beauty. Seek it in every sunset you see, every chord that is played, and every leaf that floats from a tree. Notice how this makes you feel.

Nature:

Nature is energising. Not only because of the beauty of nature, but also because of the connection we need to make with it. It is natural for us to be a part of nature. When we disconnect we cannot find the source of our energy. If we find ways to be at one with nature every day we can easily tap into a source of energy. The feeling of connecting with nature can create a physical sensation so strong that sometimes it can be misinterpreted as fear.

Exercise—Nature as an Energiser:

Make an undertaking to carry out one or more of the following during the next week:

- Take a walk alone somewhere near trees such as a wood or park.
- Plant some seeds or re-pot your house plants
- Take a trip into the countryside and sit in silence.
- Rise before dawn and watch the sun come up in the east. If you can't go outside to do this, open a window, stick your head out and watch from indoors.

Try to focus only on the activity and how it makes you feel. Put all other thoughts out of your head. Ask yourself how you feel about:

- Your health
- Your emotions
- Yourself
- Your energy

Notice the changes you feel in yourself as you carry out this activity and try to recall these as you go through the day. How does it affect your energy when you recall that moment?

You may have to keep practising this exercise until you become good at it. In particular, in letting go of all the thoughts, worries and stresses that may prey on your mind. If a thought comes into your consciousness recognise it and then let it go. It is not necessary to become angry about it. This is a part of the process. If you allow the thought to drift in and then consciously allow it to be released while you get back to your exercise you will find it becomes easier to release these undesirable thoughts at any other time during the day. Then you will be able to easily tap into the energising moment of peace that you experienced when carrying out the exercise at any time of the day.

Joy:

What fills you with joy? Joy is the greatest energiser, and yet we often forget to pursue it. We become so involved in day-to-day business that we forget to see the things that give us joy. We forget to have fun.

Fun and laughter are the greatest healers. In order to get back our ability to have fun, we need to go back to being like children, get rid of our pretensions and preconceptions and lose our inhibitions.

Fun cannot rely on approval from others. To have fun you have to fly in the face of what is socially acceptable and do it anyway. This does not mean it is essential for you to become an extrovert, rather you just need to recognise what makes for fun in your life and ensure you do it.

Fun only ever re-energises you when it does not have a detrimental affect on another. If your fun is at someone else's expense, watch out, there could be vampirism going on, and it will draw more energy from you than it will replace in the long run.

Exercise—Make work a joy:

Work can be a joy to you. Make your mind up to enjoy work, do not take yourself too seriously, but take your responsibilities to others seriously. You can be a responsible person at work and still have fun, laugh, enjoy life and get all the work done.

Share your love of life with your work colleagues, avoid gossip and enjoy absurdity. Play and be creative. Make a celebration of all your successes and a learning experience of all your so-called "failures".

Start every day by planning how the day will afford you the greatest joy possible.

Fig 7.2 Angelic Energisers:

- Get outside into nature whenever possible
- Hug someone
- Put on some happy music and dance until you drop
- Laugh. Just laugh, go on, you can do it! Ha, Ha, Ha, - that feels better already.
- Count your blessings
- Take a bath
- Take some exercise
- Do some yoga
- Meditate
- Read some inspiring verse
- Open the window and yell "Yes!" to the moon
- Discover your natural animal call; do you have one?

Exercise- Recapturing Childish Joy:

If you have children watch them at play. See if you can remember what it was like to find joy in simple pleasures. Find the joy within yourself that watching your children can bring. Try not to criticise them, and notice that your criticism of your children may relate to aspects you dislike in yourself. See only the love and joy in them, and capture that feeling. When you need to energise yourself draw out a picture of your children, or someone you love and revisit that feeling.

Exercise—Dancing for Joy:

Try putting on a happy piece of music and dancing yourself into the ground. To reenergize yourself, sing a happy song in your head, or preferably out loud. Singing at the top of your voice, no matter how well you rate it can be an energising experience.

Watch a favourite piece of comedy and practice laughing out loud. Make a point of finding everything funny, look for opportunities to laugh and share jokes, providing they are not at the expense of another person.

Physical Exercise—Walking:

Any physical activity can make you feel better and energised. But if you are not a very active person, just take a walk outside everyday. It may not be too far to begin with, in fact, if you want to make it a habit start with something you know you can easily afford to keep up.

Walking is extremely good for you, mind, body and soul. We can walk off our worries and problems. It is a great opportunity to connect with someone else. In my business, we have many of our meetings during or after a walk. We sometimes walk and talk, then stop at a picnic bench and make any notes or plans before heading back to the office.

Walking with children is a lovely way to begin the day, and it is a great investment in your relationship. If you have children, try walking to school with them rather than jumping into the car. This can start the whole family's day off well.

Summary:

Do not allow the Corrupter Vampire to take over by keeping aware of your own behaviour all the time.

We have to make a decision to open the door to joy, because although it may be tap-tap-tapping, frequently we do not hear it against all the noise in our lives. When we look for the simple pleasures and allow joy to permeate our world things change, relationships improve and love comes more easily.

MOSAIC Approach:	Examples:
Mission What do I want to achieve?	To live moment by moment in joy.
Opportunity for improvement identified. What areas in my life could do with improvement and change?	I could increase my joy by eliminating leisure activities that are "painful" especially negative TV programmes.
Skills and abilities are assessed What am I able to do, what will require practice?	I love to have a laugh and enjoy myself. I will have to practice avoiding miserable TV programmes.
Atmosphere is assessed What are things like around me? How supportive are family/friends/colleagues?	I have a lot of friends, but I do not see them as often as I could. I have some good colleagues at work
Impact of changes are considered Will there be problems, if so what are they likely to be and can I deal with them?	It will mean a change in my habits, and I may find that I slip into old ways because it seems easier. I need to prepare some treats to celebrate my successes and to keep me going.
Catalyst What can I do to speed changes into place? What will work as a catalyst for me?	Working with a friend, and perhaps having a "swear box" to fine ourselves when we slip into gossip or misery and spend it on having fun, perhaps giving a treat to someone who needs it .

"Change Thinking" Assignments

Think about the moment you are in right now. Do this as often as possible through out the day, reminding yourself, "I am alive, in this wonderful moment. All things will pass, good and bad, and therefore I will live this moment in joy".	
Begin everyday by counting your blessings, and keep doing this at regular moments throughout the day.	
Waking Mantra:	
I can find joy in every moment of my life, and with every person with whom I come into contact.	

"Take Action" Assignments

Stop watching the TV last thing at night and put on some soothing music.	
Get outside everyday and breathe in the beauty of nature around you—even if you live in a town, look for the birds, trees, plants in the gardens and window boxes	
Make an effort to hug someone every single day at least once.	
Laugh heartily at least 10 times every day—regardless of whether there is anything to laugh at!	

The Angel of Joy

Chapter 8

Step 2- Angel of Passion

Discover:
How to antidote the Intimidating Vampire
How to cure yourself of thoughts that haunt you and heal your heart

How to antidote the Intimidating Vampire.

I can be my own Guardian Angel, opening my heart to love and knowing I will be cared for by me. As I discover my true inner passions I access an endless source of loving energy.

Passion and Compassion:

The Intimidating Vampire is the bully. It will try to get its own way by beating you into submission. The inner vampire will terrorise you with thoughts, will create mental arguments and deep inner anger. This vampire is represented by the mental images we carry around within our minds of the people who have abused, scorned or upset us.

When this vampire is working within us we can feel fearful. The greatest fear is of ourselves. We may find the perpetual anxiety that we feel prevents us from getting to sleep at night. We may be on the edge of anger at any given moment, people annoy us easily, and we fly off the handle at the least provocation. We scorn ourselves, and can launch into a tirade of abuse aimed at our own supposed stupidity. We try to analyse our way out of situations, but come back home to the same thing "I created this mess, I must be to blame." This feeling of self-reproach makes us feel worse, we become confused and irrational. Life becomes a huge challenge, just getting out of bed in the morning can be hard work.

We may throw ourselves into aspects of our lives where we feel we are safe, where the vampire may not haunt us again. But, if we are to do this we have to work doubly hard to keep the thoughts at bay. Perhaps we become work orientated to avoid partners at home, or frequently sick to avoid issues at work. Our Intimidating Vampire may use anger to mask passion. When we work from our passion we throw our heart and soul into our work, relationships and life. The Intimidating Vampire undermines this by abusing this energy for its own ends.

It is only when we can feel compassion within and express passion without, learning to care for ourselves and others, that we free ourselves of the Intimidating Vampire.

How do we antidote the Intimidating Vampire within?

The antipathy to anger and hatred is compassion and care. If we are to antidote the Intimidating Vampire, we need to 'throw the holy water' at it, we need to wash it clean of its anger and reconnect it with its authentic feelings. We need to use the health and vital properties of garlic to purify the vampire's red hot blood.

Holy Water tends to burn the Intimidating Vampire, in other words, our

---

Fig 8.1 Maggie: Banishing The Inner Vampire

Maggie was 28 years old and a size 18. Maggie hated herself fat. She would either avoid looking in a mirror at all, or find herself addicted to standing in front of it berating herself. She would criticise and insult herself every time she "slipped" and came off her diet, and then she would feel so bad she would eat a bar of chocolate and the cycle would repeat. Maggie wore clothes that hid her body under folds of fabric and long dresses and jumpers. She had never had a boyfriend, and her loneliness tortured her and made her feel under greater pressure to lose weight .

She was at her lowest ebb when, on visiting her mother, Cynthia, she discovered her collapsed on the floor. At the hospital she was told that Cynthia had had a minor heart attack. Facing the mortality of her mother brought quite a few things into sharp focus for Maggie, and also for Cynthia.

Cynthia quickly recovered and on one visit she called over a favourite male nurse to meet Maggie, insisting on introducing Maggie as her "beautiful daughter". The male nurse took Maggie's hand and said that she was indeed "very lovely". Maggie was livid. "What did you call me that for?" she demanded, and Cynthia replied, "Because you are beuatiful and always have been". Then Cynthia cried and told Maggie that it hurt her badly that Maggie could not just love being herself. Cynthia asked Maggie to do her one favour. To go home and look at herself and see what she, Cynthia, sees.

At home, Maggie stood naked in front of the mirror. Was she really lovely? She collapsed on a bedroom chair and then laughed at how she looked like a Rubens figure, only needing a couple of cherubs to complete the picture. Then the transformation took place. Maggie decided she would be a Rubens model. Why not? They were considered beautiful. She went shopping and bought clothes that she had always wanted to wear but dared not. She had a chic hair cut, wore makeup and enjoyed every moment of being big and beautiful.

The next time Maggie visited her mother the male nurse asked her out, and she accepted. Maggie never has any trouble finding men to date her now!

---

immediate reaction is to get more angry, and although we say we are angry with "him" or "her" in reality we are angry with ourselves, and refusing to see it. Again, this is an example of us failing to recognise our own inner vampire. But if we allow ourselves to apply holy water consistently to our pains it should eventually cool the anger or the hot-headed emotions and enable us to reach the compassion beneath.

The Holy Water represents pure reality. It is truth; the truth we so frequently do not want to see. We may spend time trying to prove to ourselves that it was "his or her fault"; we may even relive episodes in our lives so that we can demonstrate to ourselves how wrong "he or she" was.

We expend all this effort and energy into finding a reason for getting angry with ourselves.

How to cure yourself of thoughts that haunt you and heal your heart

If it is no longer present, and yet this vampire is still draining us, we know that we are vampirising ourselves. We must stop "eating our hearts out" and begin to heal ourselves. Our heart will become healed when we are able to discover the true passion that lies within it. Then we can surrender to this passion and yield to the flow of life and to the love that will flow to us.

Awakening the Angel of Passion—Motivation vs. Passion:
In order to understand passion we need to be clear about the difference between this and motivation. One of the enduring and simplest theories about motivation is Abraham Maslow's pyramid or Hierarchy of Human Needs. This represents our basic needs in the order at which they manifest themselves and explains how we are motivated to satisfy each need in turn (see fig 8.2).

Initially, we tend to be motivated solely for the satisfaction of the first human need and until we have achieved this we do not concern ourselves with any others. We climb the pyramid as, on satisfaction of each need, we tend to strive for the next.

At the base of the pyramid are the most basic needs. Food, water and warmth, our requirements that enable us to survive. These provide our most basic motivation. This motivation becomes a driving force and shapes all our actions until it is satisfied. Until these needs are satisfied we will not be motivated by anything but the need to attain them.

The second stage of the pyramid is that of Security. When we have attained adequate food, water and warmth (physiological needs), then we will begin to want for some safety or security. At this point perhaps we would be looking for accommodation that will offer protection to us.

The third level reflects our need for human company. Only when we have attained these basic requirements do we actively seek other beings. It is at this point that we would desire companionship.

Companionship eventually gives rise to competitiveness, as we then become motivated to achieve some level of status within our social group.

Self realisation is our final motivation. Having achieved a sense of status as the boss of the company, 'the chief of the tribe', we then consider 'self actualisation'. This is the need for an innate purpose, a desire to develop as people, to understand ourselves and our place within the universe.

Comparing passion and motivation:

From the comparisons (fig 8.3i-iii) we can see that:

- Motivation is an external force.
- Passion is an internal force.

In other words, we are motivated by the circumstances that surround us, the environment and our needs. Passion, on the other hand, is from within, it is something we feel, and may not be able to give clear reasons for. Both passion

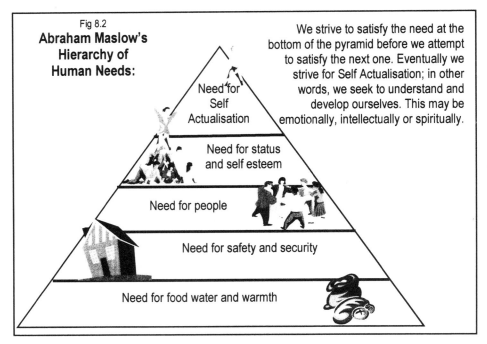

Fig 8.2
Abraham Maslow's Hierarchy of Human Needs:

We strive to satisfy the need at the bottom of the pyramid before we attempt to satisfy the next one. Eventually we strive for Self Actualisation; in other words, we seek to understand and develop ourselves. This may be emotionally, intellectually or spiritually.

Need for Self Actualisation

Need for status and self esteem

Need for people

Need for safety and security

Need for food water and warmth

Fig 8.3i **The Difference between Motivation and Passion**	
Motivation	**Passion**
Depends on the **circumstances** of the person, such as where they are on Maslow's Pyramid.	Depends upon the **feelings** of the person
Tends to be generic, following a pattern. In other words, we often know what kinds of things will be motivating, such as money, time, fun etc	Can be individual, even unique, varies according to the person. We can never be sure what someone feels passionate about.
You can try to motivate someone, and sometimes you can succeed.	You either feel passionate or you do not. It is difficult to make someone feel passionate about something.
Motivation comes from external forces.	Passion comes from within.

and motivation are driving forces. However, it is passion that gives us the greatest energy. When we are working from our passion we have enormous quantities of energy, greater amounts than we could imagine possible. We are able to achieve more without feeling exhausted.

When does passion become obsession?
Consider someone who is a "workaholic". There is no joy in a person addicted to their work. They do it because they feel they have to. They have no control. This does not mean they perform well. In fact they can have impaired judgement as a result of sleeplessness and long working hours.

When people feel passionate about their work they also give themselves time to recuperate in order to perform well. They have a lot of energy and invest fun in the job.

When we are addicted we are vampires. Passion is an angelic quality. It is important that we are able to identify our own passions in life, as when we allow this angel to awaken we will discover our lost energy and become able to create better relationships. A person in whom there is no vestige of passion will only create vampiric relationships. Finding and living your passion is essential to awakening that angel within you and within your relationships.

Finding your Passion:

There are different types of passion, but the common denominator is that they affect the persons inner being. In other words, they may feel elevated by participating and some people consider this a spiritual experience. A persons passion has a sense of "higher purpose", of importance. Passion makes people feel they are closer to their true nature or inner self.

Some may not be true "passions" as they are really an addiction to an adrenaline rush, or excitement. Football may be a case in point. Likewise, parachuting or other thrill sports. On the other hand, flying (e.g. hang gliding) may evoke a feeling of calm and may be considered a passion as it creates a deep sense of self. Only you can honestly say if you feel passion.

When Passion becomes the Grouch Bear:

The Grouch Bear is another aspect of the Vampire. The Grouch Bear is moody and unresponsive, it wants to hide away and when it is disturbed it can be dangerous. It is like a bear with a sore head. The Grouch Bear does not actively intimidate; it does so passively. It waits for someone to say something, anything, but this will be the "wrong" thing and then it will complain or attack.

Grouch Bears think that everyone else is deliberately annoying them. They will tell you that you spoke out of turn, and then quote back what you said, but making your words sound aggressive. If you recognise this you may be a Grouch Bear yourself.

Fig 8.3ii **External and Internally Orientated Passions:**

Initiated from the world around us—Externally Orientated:
These passions are often with a moral bias, in other words, it is something you believe in,such as a passion for a belief or practice, a charity or good works etc.

Initiated from within us—Internally Orientated:
These usually fall into one of three categories:

- Aesthetic – in other words, to do with beauty such as creative or artistic pursuits etc. This may even include gardening or architecture.
- Developmental – that is, anything to do with learning more about yourself or the world around you, developing new skills.
- Experiential – which means, having a passion for new experiences which may include travelling. But this does not necessarily include "thrill" orientated experiences as these can be an addiction to the adrenaline rush.

Fig 8.3iii **Comparing Obsession and Addiction with Passion**	
Obsession and Addiction	**Passion**
You may notice that people who are addicted are often: • Tired • Irritable • Driven (I **have to** finish this…, I have to stay in this relationship etc) • Unhappy with their work/life • Able to discuss nothing else • Stressed • Worried • Feel out of control • Joyless • Make life/work sound dull • Have little energy	People who are passionate about their work: • Have fun • Enjoy themselves • Feel pleased about what they are doing • Want to do what they feel passionate about all the time for the joy of it • Feel their passion is the best thing in their lives • Are able to have other interests and friendships • Are not boring • Are full of energy • Recognise that they need time to be alone to recharge • Do not worry about life

Remember that bears like sweet things, they love honey, and that Grouch Bears are no exception. Say nice things to your own inner Grouch Bear, because Bears are not good at giving up their suppers, and have been known to steal. Therefore, make sure your own Bear is well fed with nourishing and loving thoughts and words. Tell yourself nice things about you, without comparing to the other grouch Bear in your life. Remember that a Grouch Bear can only remain in the company of other Grouch Bears. Once all the Bears have left it will leave too, eventually.

Once you have fed your own Bear, give your partner's Grouch Bear something sweet, say loving, and non judgemental, things and he or she may return to being an Angel again quite quickly.

The Guardian Angel:

The Guardian Angel is our unique self-protection system. It is this angel who provides us with inner support and approval. This angel carries us through difficulties by reminding us of our vision, reminding of us of whom we really are, and that we are not just the sum of our debts, or the status of our job or "quality" of our friends.

Truth about ourselves::

The Guardian brings us back to some home truths about ourselves:

- That we are valuable
- That we require protection
- That we should be cared for
- That we are worthy of love

How we can abuse the Guardian Angel:

We can be our own Guardian Angel when we stop trying to beat it down and beat it up. The Guardian Angel is often blamed for everything that goes wrong in our lives. It is a strange twist that we turn upon the very angel that could be providing us with support and protection. We turn upon ourselves.

The Face of the Vampire:

When we have been dealt a blow in love or life it can leave a lasting impression on the mind. This can cause us a great deal of pain. There are many strategies that we can employ. For example, we may:

- Try "not to think about it", block it out
- Relive the situations that created the pain again and again
- Talk incessantly, finding anyone who will be a listening ear
- Talk to the "wrong people" and fail to confide in the ones who are most trustworthy
- Wallow in our grief

These behaviours can create thoughts that haunt us. We feel as though we cannot escape from this nightmarish existence; our stomach lurches, our hands shake and the hairs on the back of our necks may stand on end just at the merest thought of the vampire who has attacked and controlled us.

The face of the vampire is clear in our minds, and its haunting presence can affect everything about the way we live our lives, where we go, what we do, who we meet; we become prisoners in a life that struggles to exclude any contact with our attacker, and all the while, we are the ones who suffer. We lose our friends, we become isolated and lonely, and this vampire gets an ever-increasing stronghold in our minds.

When we are stalked and attacked by vampires we can feel haunted by them in our waking and sleeping lives. We think about the vampire time and time again, never coming to a satisfactory solution in our minds. The vampire seems to live on within us, even when we have moved forward in our lives and, physically and/or emotionally, left them behind.

The vampire continues to live within us, and all the while it is weaving a destructive magic over our lives. No matter how far away it is the spell continues to entrance us.

We can be more afraid of this vampire when it exists only within our thoughts than when it is close at hand. Once the vampire has seeped into our brains its presence seems more pernicious than its reality ever was.

The Angel beneath the mask of the vampire:

The vampire within is only a mask, and beneath this hideous mask is no one other than ourselves. For no one but us exists within our own mind. Every character we create within ourselves is a part of ourselves. The vampire you make within you is no more than an aspect of yourself; one you may not like to look at, but it is you none the less.

Healing the heart:

In order to keep healthy we need to maintain a healthy balance of energy, so that there is a flow inwards and outwards.

When we are dealt a blow in love or relationships there can be a tendancy to "close ourselves off", instead of remaining open, and choose power over love. The technique to employ with vampires is to "be love" and not "give love". This disempowers them, as they are unable to feed unless you open your jugular and offer it.

Existing in love, means we can find our own source of energy from our sense of who we are, without needing others to validate us.

Energy of the Heart:

Do you feel you are moving to a healthy beat? Does your life feel "bunged up" with trifles or annoyances that keep your from what matters most?

To quote Patch Adams, the "Red-Nosed Doctor", "passion is a kind of surrender". In other words, passion is not something you have to find within, develop, force, motivate. Passion exists.

A passion exists within us all. But a passion for what? In order to go with the flow of change we need to surrender to our passion. When we surrender to our passion we *will* be working at the "pace of change". The energy of our passion can create changes in our lives that allow us to reach the next level.

Fig 8.4 **Unmasking the Vampire**

At the time I was furious with a particular vampire for the way it had affected my life. I was haunted by thoughts of it running round my head, and every time my stomach would turn over and I would feel myself flushing. I felt quite ill.

I tried to avoid the issue, blocking it out of my mind, but instead it became a bigger and bigger "bogey" until I knew I had to go through the process of unmasking the vampire.

Once I had lifted the mask I was amazed by the outcome of this process. Beneath the vampire I found that there was a small and vulnerable child. It was me, at about four years old. I asked her what she really wanted and this little girl told me that she needed a hug.

Suddenly, it all became clear to me. Once I saw it was just me under there all the time, and I was able to find out what this little girl needed I realised that I was able to heal my heart. I had been attacking myself; every time I berated the vampire, I was really running myself down, castigating myself for being so useless and vulnerable. No wonder the little girl was hiding.

When I saw her little face, I could see the fear and desperate need to be loved by someone bigger and stronger that was in her eyes, just as it can be in any child. I stopped seeing that part of me as an adult, and realised that it was still in need of care and protection; while all I had been doing was attacking it and making it feel unlovable and unworthy.

I had to learn to love the angel behind the vampire. I have had to remove the vampire mask from time to time, when it hides my angel, but I no longer feel haunted by vampires.

Positive Projecting:

Frequently we will project upon others, in other words, we see in the other person our own feelings, jealousies, insecurities, doubts etc. We are also unaware of doing it. We believe the feelings we are attaching to the other person are completely genuine. We often do not even recognise that we have these feelings at all.

To heal our hearts we need to project positively. Imagine that the person we are blaming for our pain feels exactly the same as we do. Imagine that for a moment; contemplate that the very person who has given us this pain feels the same about us as we do about him or her. What is your first reaction?

Often it is, "how can s/he feel the same as me, I am the injured party!" If this is your thinking then I am afraid I have only one assumption to make, that you have allowed your vampire to rise. If, instead, you are able to follow this possibility, no matter how difficult it feels, then, there is hope that you can cure yourself and heal your heart. This is the Holy Water.

The Holy Water is the sprinkling of common sense upon the heart. Pure truth. Unless we can recognise that others feel similar to ourselves, we cannot deal with reality. We, instead, "create" reality as we would like it to be, not as it is, and continue to be dissatisfied by our inability to do anything about it.

Exercise: Stand before the mirror.

To heal you heart you need to get to some home truths. Stand before the mirror and talk to yourself as though you were talking to the person with whom you have the grievance.

Now imagine *they* are saying these things to *you*. How do you feel? It is likely that you will be feeling hurt, or most likely it will seem incredible—"How could s/he possibly say that about me when it is so patently untrue!"

Now, just accept it as true for a moment. Ask yourself, "What if it was true about me?" What would you do? What would you expect?

When we have accepted that the faults that we see clearly in others are really just bringing up things within ourselves that need to be dealt with, then we can heal. It is not possible to heal if you want to hold onto the disease. However hurt, aggrieved or furious you feel, until you realise that you created these feelings and until you are prepared to let go of them and accept that you have a large part to play in them, you will not get better. You cannot cure yourself of a disease whilst wanting to hold onto and love the very virus that causes it.

Attracting Love into our Lives:

To attract love, we need only to "be love". That means we need to think and act "in love" or "with love". Everything we say and do needs to come from a place of love within our hearts. This thaws us and protects us from Emotional Hypothermia. While we remain open our hearts do not chill, and instead their capacity for love expands and our heart grows with it.

Remember "The Grinch" in "How The Grinch Stole Christmas" by Dr Seuss. He could not take part in the fun and joviality of Christmas because "his heart was too tight". When it grew a little he was able to give love and immediately attracted love into his world. Simple fables like this usually hold the most profound truths. Love more and receive more joy.

Facing the "Enemy" with Compassion:

Here we can refer to the Taoist principal Wu Wei. Wu Wei means "without doing, causing or making". In other words, without interfering, tampering and generally sticking your oar in. Wu Wei is the water flowing downstream, it does not try to flow in a straight line, it flows around and between the rocks that stand in its way.

In the martial arts, the Wu Wei approach is to wear out the opponent by deflecting his energy or sending it back to him; responding to an attack by yielding. This can be demonstrated by imagining a floating cork. The harder you hit it the more it yields and the greater force with which it pops back up.

Fig 8.5 Angelic Voices Case Study - Yielding:

I was aware of an Intimidating Vampire, the Finance Director, on the war path, making her way straight for the door of my office. I was having a meeting at the time with two managers. When she entered she immediately began by shouting and waving a piece of paper at me. The problem apparently was the poor quality of work my staff were carrying out, demonstrated by the forms that were being incorrectly completed.

I sat back in my chair and, when there was a break in the tirade, I asked her simply to specify the problem in detail. I told her I did not have an answer to the complaint, because I would have to investigate it. I continued to be relaxed and spoke very quietly.

After a few moments she stopped shouting and began to speak in a civilised tone. We completed the discussion with me telling her I would talk to her when my current meeting had completed and I had looked into things a little more. She left.

The two managers with whom I was meeting looked at me with a mixture of admiration and surprise, they were aware of this vampire's methods, and both congratulated me on remaining cool and calm. They commented that my coolness, even in the face of no evidence or argument completely disarmed the vampire.

I felt really pleased because I did not lose any energy on the exchange.

We can use this in conflict resolution, instead of trying to fight back, or to find a clever response, we allow the negative energy to flow over us, and, like the stream, we flow with it. The secret is to flow, reflect and then respond, and the response should always be with compassion. In this way we yield to the attack and pop up with greater force by being compassionate.

Yielding to the Inner Vampire:

Yielding is all about going with the flow; in other words, allowing things to happen and relying on your intuition to determine what to do next. In order to do this we have to learn to trust ourselves.

Practically, this means developing a belief that we are capable of dealing with any events as they arise. In order to develop this skill, we have first to be able to go with the inner flow. When the inner vampire rises to taunt us we need to go with it, roll with the punches, and not try to close it off or suppress it. Ask yourself, "What am I really feeling about this?"

Exercise: Yielding to the Inner Vampire

This exercise can be carried out at any time in order to prepare yourself for the moments when you may think that you will need to challenge your thinking more forcefully. By preparing now, you will soon see that yielding is easy, and yet is most powerful.

Notice each de-energising thought you have as it comes up (this may be self-

doubt, self-reproach, anger, frustration, jealousy, fear etc). Every time you question, doubt or wonder, say to yourself "I yield to this thought/feeling, I allow myself to flow with this way of thinking and being".
Then notice how you feel about it?
When you go with the feeling you may have a moment of intensity; however, this is usually followed by peace of mind and stillness. Remember the cork popping up and then floating along on its way. See the case study (fig. 8.5)

Maintaining an energy flow:

We consider our thinking to be located in our head. But where is our feeling? We feel with our entire body, and we touch our heart when we want to illustrate that something moves us.
Our body has memories – for example, you may have a stiff neck because you were sitting badly as a result of completing some work that caused you stress. At the same time, you may know who or what the pain in your neck is! You can often identify the emotional hurt that is behind the physical pain.

Exercise—Holding Emotions in our Body:

Consider the following questions:
Where in the body do you feel your lack of energy? How does a lack of energy or health manifest itself for you? This will probably be different for everyone.
Consider any physical discomforts you may have and see if these correlate with your emotions? Can you identify what the pain you are feeling represents for you? Think about expressions you use -"He is a pain" "This is a headache". Do these relate to how you physically feel?

Exercise: Unmasking the Vampire

This can be a painful process, but it is also a rewarding one. At this stage we do not want to dwell on painful memories of events and people, but we need to make this one exception in order to move forward.
Think about a vampire that has haunted you. Picture the person's face in your mind. Now spend some time really imagining that person and the way in which s/he used to behave.
Think about the vampiristic behaviours s/he would use with you. In the past this may have made you angry, but on this occasion it will not. Instead you will be noticing the behaviours dispassionately, observing what is happening, the facial expressions, the covert meanings under the words spoken etc. When the experience is rich and full, imagine yourself entering the scene. You are going to confront this vampire who has lived for too long within your own mind.

Imagine approaching the vampire, getting very close indeed. Then notice that the vampire's face is nothing more than a mask that you can remove.

Reach up and pull the mask off the vampire. Who is behind it? The only person that can be behind is you. It is your brain, and it is you doing the thinking. Look at yourself. What do you look like? Are you just a small child? Ask yourself, the 'you' that was behind the mask, "What do you need?" and see what answer you get. Now you can give *yourself* the love you want.

Fig 8.6 Angelic Voices—Finding the gifts

We were under a deadline to get a massive order completed for delivery the following morning at 8.00 am. We still had an enormous amount to do and the whole team were involved with working on the computers to put together the material we needed. Everyone was rushing, but we were all pulling together. Suddenly all the power went off. The computers seemed to die. We had a power cut, and on calling the power company it was clear this would last for at least three hours. After a momentary panic we stopped and asked ourselves, "How can we use this moment well?" We decided to spend the time we could not otherwise use working on the computers, to plan, and by doing so quickly realised that by rethinking the way we worked we could cut our workload by over a half. We all took time to get our plans clarified and just as we were ready to recommence, the power came back on. The work was finished by the deadline, but looking back, we would not have succeeded if we had not seen the gift in the situation and used it well.

Exercise: The Gifts

Every experience that you have could be positive or negative. Your view of it is dependent upon your attitude. It is difficult to see something positive in some situations, but it is not impossible. Whatever happens, somewhere there is a gift. Consider some of the difficult events you have been faced with and consider the gifts that the situation contained.

Exercise: The Gifts in the Haunting

What are the thoughts that haunt you? These are the scenarios that go round and round in your mind; they may be conversations, events or a collection of feelings associated with a person, place or object.

When you find these thoughts circulating, look for the gift in the haunting. In other words, what positive results have you had since the encounter? What have you learned about yourself? When you can find the gifts you will stop repeating your mistakes. For example, when you realise that the ex-lover who is haunting your thoughts gave you an opportunity to discover your personal power and potential when s/he left you, you are less likely to go back into this unsatisfactory relationship.

How can we live without fear of vampires?

We need to be open in our relationships, and not to become sceptical about everyone's motives. If we believe we see vampires everywhere and that we must therefore protect ourselves, our own inner vampire has probably risen from the grave!

In order to exist within love, you need to find your own self worth, value yourself and suspend the need to make judgements. This requires us to stop saying that vampires are right or wrong, and justifying our own behaviours. Instead we need to find and surrender to our passion, find the approval and love we need from within, rather than projecting it upon the people around us. This creates energy self-sufficiency. Losing the need for others liberates us from any vampiric attacks.

Exercise in Affirming:

This is the most important of all. Affirming changes the way you think, the way you act and the way others behave around you. We all affirm all the time. Whatever we affirm becomes our reality. For example, we may affirm that we never have any luck with relationships; or that life is not fair.

There are many reasons that affirming affects our reality. We know that it must work on the subconscious mind.

Remember the importance of self love and acceptance. Everyday make loving and accepting affirmations; for example "I deeply and profoundly love and accept myself". No matter how strange it feels, keep practicing everyday.

Summary

Find and live your passion and you will become free of your vampires.

Everything you learn is a gift, but most especially when you learn something about yourself.

Look beneath the vampire's mask and you will find yourself.

Feed your Grouch Bears a diet of sweet thoughts and honeyed words.

MOSAIC Approach:	Examples:
Mission What do I want to achieve?	Yielding to the flow of life, yielding to my passion.
Opportunity for improvement identified. What areas in my life could do with improvement and change?	Not rising to the bait so readily when provoked.
Skills and abilities are assessed What am I able to do, what will require practice?	I know that I can avoid conflict, but that when I do, I do not feel any better about the situation. I need to practice "ignoring the nonsense" and dealing with the message.
Atmosphere is assessed What are things like around me? How supportive are family/friends/colleagues?	My biggest problem is at work, and so I need to ensure I can feel secure and perhaps be prepared when I have to face vampires. This is especially true in meetings.
Impact of changes are considered Will there be problems, if so what are they likely to be and can I deal with them?	People at work may find me less easy to "push around". I suspect that some people will not be too happy about this, I need to consider how I can ensure that this change does not create insecurity in them.
Catalyst What can I do to speed changes into place? What will work as a catalyst for me?	Preparing myself in advance of meetings, so that I am not taken off guard, as I seem to be, nearly every time!

"Change Thinking" Assignments ✓

Notice if you berate yourself and immediately alter your behaviour; say some kind and loving words to yourself.	
When life becomes challenging think to yourself—"There is a gift in every moment, what is the gift in *this* moment?" and seek then it out.	
Waking Mantra:	
I am living my passion now and in every moment.	

"Take Action" Assignments ✓

"Ignore the nonsense" and respond to the message.	
Make all your dealings with people "compassionate".	
When we are obsessed with thoughts of a vampire, look within and unmask the angel.	
Use positive projection to learn to accept others for who they are, and concentrate our efforts on fixing ourselves instead.	
Feed your Grouch bear on sweet words, especially "I love you".	

Chapter 9

Step 3 - Angel of Freedom

Discover:
How to antidote the Needy Vampire.
How to become immune to the fear of rejection.

How to antidote the Needy Vampire

By learning how to let go of our attachment to the world we are able to rise above it, and feel as though we are free and flying, we no longer need to manipulate to avoid rejection, and we are no longer rejected.

Soaring:
The Angel of Freedom represents our angel when it is soaring. When we harness this angelic influence we are able to take off. We feel as though we are flying high and yet without the fear of falling. We can achieve this when we allow the angel to support us and release our grasp on the earth.

The Angel of Freedom is spontaneous; it does not use patterns of communication that create vampirism. It is free of the need to conform to ways that dissatisfy, and it brings love and joy into the lives of everyone it touches.

Letting go of our need for a relationship allows us to discover its true value, and the value of both our partner and ourselves.

We often resist letting go because it creates anxiety within us. As babies we had to learn how to let go of the hand that guided us, and yet many of us seek to grasp at something or someone else in order to feel secure.

We try to build relationships by attachments, frequently these are detrimental to both individuals, as, in order to hold on to our partners, we use methods and means that force or manipulate them. We remain bound together because we fear being apart, we blame our partner for our failure to be self-supporting, and yet we are setting him/her up as a vampire.

Expectations in relationships create unnecessary pressures, and are usually complex and almost impossible to rationalise. We create a convoluted set of rules as to what is or is not acceptable according to our mood at the time. We expect our partner to be able to read these differing rules and choose the right one at the right time. When s/he fails to do so it is an opportunity for us move back into judgement and blame.

Needing Attachment

Needy Vampires need attachment. When we feel vulnerable within the world it is because we attach our security to something. It may be to money, or to a partner, to a job or to friendships. Whatever it is, the need to create attachments leaves us feeling as though we are clinging on for dear life.

When we look about us, we may see some people who seem to soar above problems, they do not have money worries; they do not feel lonely without a partner or any real friends. These people appear to fly on angelic wings.

Perhaps we see our parents in this way, so that they are always there to bail us out when we get things wrong, or when we foul up our latest relationship, or lose all our money on a "get rich quick scheme".

The Needy part of us will require continual reaffirmation. That is, it must be told that it is loved and cared for. When we live with this Vampire within us we will always be asking, "Do you love me"? We will also be counting the number of times we are told, "I love you" to see if it is sufficient. And of course, it will never be enough. We will demand reassurance at all times. We ask ourselves "Have I been reassured that I am loved recently?", because we want to be told constantly.

When we are within the Needy Vampire state we will say "I love you" because we want to hear our partner say "I love you too". If they do not reply with this we feel aggrieved, or hurt or angry. This is the basis of the expectations we

---

 Fig 9.1 Angelic Voices—**Sarah and Ben:**

Sarah loved Ben looking after her, and Ben would enjoy demonstrating how much he loved her. He would pop out to the shops if ever anything was needed for the evening meal, or for any other domestic requirements; he did most errands. Sarah rarely left the house. If she felt she wanted something she could just ask Ben and he would be delighted to go.

Ben would help Sarah prepare for any journey she was going on without him: maps, directions and all the things she may need for the trip. Ben ran the house, he would remind Sarah of what she needed for work, pack her lunches and even remind her of calls she needed to make to her mother or friends. Every now and again Ben would lose his temper without knowing why. Sarah would find Ben maddening, her friends thought Ben was wonderful and so did not sympathise.

Ben had succeeded in activating Sarah's vampire, and she had become dependent upon his energy. Through a concerted effort she determined to tell Ben that she loved him, but that she could handle things on her own. She took the initiative and, surprisingly, found herself quite nervous about venturing out to the shops alone. Slowly her confidence returned and their marriage was saved. Now they both contribute to their domestic bliss in their own ways, but are aware when they are beckoning vampire in each other from the grave.

have within our relationships, the demands that we make upon others, the methods by which we set people up to fail us, so that we can complain about the injustice of it all.

How do we antidote the Needy Vampire within?

When we antidote the Needy Vampire we no longer measure the love we are given, we accept that we are loved. Love is not something that we seek from the outside, we know it exists and live in harmony with it on the inside.

The more we are able to awaken and live with this inner love, the more we find that it draws to it the love of others. We no longer trade our love for another; we give and let go of receiving. We no longer need to know that we are appreciated, because we know that we appreciate ourselves, and that this has greatest value of all.

If we are to slay the Needy Vampire, we must "cut off its head". This will neutralise a vampire, whereas cutting off any other limbs will have no effect. This can be seen, almost amusingly, in the Andy Wahol film "Blood for Dracula". In this, Dracula chases our hero, who tries to cut him down with an axe. Successive limbs are severed as Dracula continues to attack and pursue, it is only when his head is finally cut off that the vampire dies.

Cutting off the head and suspending belief:

The only way we can get our angel off the ground is when we suspend belief. It was considered impossible that man should fly, and yet some people decided to reject that. As a result the Wright Brothers invented the first airplane. They suspended belief, they did not listen to the "accepted wisdom" of the day, instead they chose to turn their backs on "logic and knowledge" and turned instead to inspiration and creativity. They freed themselves of the limiting ideas of the times and freely imagined possibilities that would soon become reality.

The only way we can do the same is to disconnect our thinking, and so allow ourselves to work from the intuition, or instinct, or with what our heart tells us. When we remove our brain (figuratively) we stop trying to manipulate and just feel, we do not need to decide how we feel about something or someone, we just experience the feeling.

How to become immune to the fear of rejection.

Our fears of rejection are false. We cannot be rejected when we accept ourselves.

The Queen of Hearts:

The Needy Vampire can become the Queen of Hearts. The Queen of Hearts believes she has suffered a greater pain than anyone else. Only The Queen of Hearts knows how bad and sad life is and she carries the burden of her pain; she believes that only she is worthy of carrying this pain, others are insensitive to her, uncaring, self-obsessed or simply luckier than she.

The Queen of Hearts carries her pain like a trophy before her, she shows it to people from time to time, or it may be the great unspoken issue. And in either case it holds tremendous power, and so does she.

Off With Her Head:

You may recall the Queen of Hearts from "Alice's Adventures in Wonderland". The whole of Wonderland was afraid of this creature, afraid, that is, of causing her offence. They bowed and scraped to no avail in many cases; if the Queen did not approve of you she had you be-headed.

This caricature represents the worst side of us when we are in the Queen of Hearts mode. We can threaten our friendships, our partnerships— if we are not satisfied, if we are not appeased we will say "Off with your head!"

The friendship must end, the partnership is over, we can never speak to him or her again. We threaten our friends with this dire consequence if they fail us by not behaving in the way that we think they should. We heap upon them our own rules, our own expectation of what makes a good or poor friend, and then "WHAM" if they dare to "upset" us, we terminate the relationship.

Of course, he or she may apologise to us, and as the Queen of Hearts, we will only accept the most humble of apologies, and then we will make sure that he or she fully understands the depth of the pain that he or she caused us. At that point we may be willing to reconsider the friendship.

By this time our friends may have decided we are not worth the bother, our partners may seek comfort elsewhere, and all this will demonstrate to us just how little people will care for us, how easy it is to abandon us.

Fear of Abandonment:

The Queen of Hearts fears abandonment most of all. And yet she is most likely to experience it. Her ability to push people away is only exceeded by her ability to feel let down by them.

The challenge that the Queen sets down is: If you love me prove it by fulfilling my expectations. These will be great, and it will be your personal quest to ensure you succeed. If you do not succeed it will mean that you will not love me enough, and it will be a good job that I discovered it.

However, at the same time the Queen gives her partner opportunities to be humble, which allows her to feel more attached and less likely to be abandoned. When our partner throws himself or herself to the floor we feel more secure, but not for long.

Unfortunately, the Queen's fear of abandonment is a constant, it does not go away no matter how many different quests or tournaments her subjects participate in. She is a prisoner of the pack, trapped in her role, as much as any other card.

Making rules for relationships:

When we are playing the Queen of Hearts we will make up rules for our relationships and insist upon people working within these rules. We will tell those people with whom we have our relationship that they must do things in a certain way if they are to please us. If they fail, they are for the guillotine. Examples of these rules may be that people must always be honest, must not be late, must always ask me out first, must never go out with my ex-boyfriends/ex-girlfriends etc.

A pack of cards:

We all have a Queen of Hearts, whether we are male of female. She is at once terrifying and pathetic and like the Queen in Alice in Wonderland, she is fickle and will need constant reassurance. The King of Hearts tried very hard to please his wife, but he was always onto a loser.

Alice observed that the Queen was just a playing card, she had no substance, she was only two dimensional, and was really not capable of meting out the punishments she enjoyed threatening. "You are nothing but a pack of cards!" Alice told her, heralding, or perhaps even evoking, the end of her dream.

The Queen is part of a pack of cards. She is worthless unless she is with the pack, she has no currency alone, it is only when compared to the others that she has value.

No Freedom in being Queen:

A Queen has apparent freedom, but in reality is almost a prisoner of her position. The film Roman Holiday, starring Audrey Hepburn and Gregory Peck provides a wonderful insight into this, as Hepburn plays the Princess who absconds for a wonderful day of freedom as a "normal" girl and as such is able to soar by discovering her true self. As a result she changes from being more or less a child, dependent upon the approval and management of her "Court", to controlling her own destiny.

However, in a pack of cards all the characters are all two faced! To be free we need to break out of the pack and go with our inner self, discover who we are and let go of the self-sabotage that builds our fragile and hierarchical house of cards. We do not need to keep things "together". When we release the Queen she is able to discover that flying on the wind is much more fun and does not demand courtiers in attendance.

Relationships On Trial:

Alice was her own Queen of Hearts, and as such she was trying to sabotage herself. Until she rejected this the Queen maintained power, Alice was afraid of her, and even stood up in her Court of Law. A strange court where the Queen made up the rules as she went along.

This is typical of the courts within which we try our friends, colleagues and partners. We set up the procedures on a basis that appears fair, but then change the way we carry out the procedure if it does not meet with our ways.

When we set rules we make it difficult for people to succeed in caring for us without having to measure their loyalty or love against a scale that we have devised for ourselves.

Fig 9.2 **Warding off vampires within the home:**

In the home, we can banish vampires by:

- Freely providing support for each other.
- Recognising the needs you have in yourself before letting the vampire rise from the grave.
- Preventing yourself from "unloading our troubles" upon your partner without ensuring you have a source of energy to draw upon. For example, if you want to talk through problems, go for a walk and get into some fresh air, this helps to reduce the exhausting effect.
- Do not offer solutions to your partner, allow him/her unloading time, then ask if s/he wants ideas. If you offer solutions too readily you may become a victim of vampirism through the "yes but.." response. In this situation no solution will be acceptable because the partner may require love and approval and not ideas.
- Demonstrate love frequently, through touch, cuddles and loving words.
- Do not be afraid to say how you feel when you are weakened or vulnerable. Ask for what you really want.

Fig 9.3 Angelic Voices—Case Study: Bill

After Bill and Rose had been going out together for five years Rose ended the relationship. It was a huge shock to Bill, as he thought they would be getting married that year.

After a while Bill began to date again, but he could not lose the attachment to Rose. When he met Claudia he felt she could be the girl for him, but she felt that she was always fighting against the "memory" Bill had of Rose. Twice Bill called Claudia by Rose's name. On the second occasion Claudia told Bill that there had always been three people in their relationship, and that that was one too many. She left him, saying that with the other woman in his life her going would not leave him "on his own".

Bill realised that Rose had become an inner vampire and that he was really afraid of being abandoned. His fear had created the thing he most dreaded. Bill created a life for himself and managed to awaken his angel. After a while he found that he did not need anyone in his life. Amazingly, as soon as he made this declaration a new woman literally knocked on his door. Pamela, an old school friend, had looked him up because she was in the neighbourhood. They have been married for ten blissful years and have twin girls of four years old.

Awakening the Angel of Freedom:

The Angel of Freedom does not need attachment. By freeing itself from the need to attach an emotion to a person or a thing, it is able to feel any emotion it wants, because its emotions come from within. This is represented by an angel in flight.

The angel in flight does not have any strings attached, it does not have a safety net, it simply soars above our heads, trusting implicitly in its ability to remain airborne regardless of the environment. As this angel is free it does not heap expectations upon others, it is liberated from these; they hold it down like cables that hold down a hot air balloon before it is released. The weight of expectations is a burden that would pin it to the ground.

All expectations are put upon ourselves. When others expect things from us we choose whether or not we are going to fulfil their expectation, whether we will buy into it, or not.

Off with your own head!

If we are to rid ourselves of the Queen of Hearts we can become three-dimensional beings, we no longer have to be a part of a pack of cards. In other words, we have to cut off our own heads. We need to disconnect our brains and allow ourselves to feel our feelings. In this way we stop the endless analysis and internal talk, and instead notice what we are feeling and go with our intuition. We work from the heart, finding our authentic feelings and responding to these.

When we remove our heads we stop thinking "is it possible?" and just do it. Our angel does not worry about whether it will fall when it leaps from the mountain; instead it trusts its instincts and knows it will be suspended in mid air.

When we are no longer attached to the past, present or future, to people, objects and events we are free, we can tune into our potential, and we do not need to cling onto the mountainside. We discover that we are perfect and whole and that the universe supports us entirely.

Our fear of abandonment is an archaic response from our babyhood. At this age we had to be cared for by our mothers or carers, because we were vulnerable and dependant and without her we would have died.

Now we are adult, those fears no longer serve us.

Cut off the Thinking:

The head is the home of thought. Too much thinking causes us to lose contact with our feelings; the heart becomes disconnected from the mind. When this happens we rationalise what we are feeling in order to disassociate ourselves from the emotion.

Emotional feelings can be extremely strong and, in an attempt to maintain "control", the mind decides whether this is acceptable or not to the whole person. The mind, being the intellectual and therefore rational and logical part, will often decide that the emotion does not fit its picture of balance, and so will suppress the emotion. However, the "logic" upon which these decisions are founded is flawed.

Thinking vs. Feeling—Science as the new Gods:

If the mind were to consider the value of the emotions then it would understand logically that they are a necessary part of the whole person, instead the mind becomes overwhelmed by its own importance. Emotions are considered to be "in the way" rather than a benefit to our development.

This is promoted by the way in which our modern society values only logical empirical thought. The word empiric relates to the ability to test and duplicate. Empirical science rejects anything that cannot be proven in theory and practice. We have come to "believe in" science as though it holds all the answers, in the way that our forebears believed in their Gods, whether they be Christian, pagan or otherwise.

We cannot prove love scientifically, however that does not mean it does not exist, and so empirical science is not always a useful method for measuring value or truth. Love is a good example of a concept that is real and true for us all, and yet is impossible to measure or prove. The problem of science is that it tends to disconnect us from our feelings. Therefore, when this thinking is prevalent it is essential to reconnect to the heart.

Without a strong heart and mind connection we are only half a person, and therefore we feel lacking. This sense of lacking is the basis of the vacuum that prompts our desire for energy, and may lead to vampirism.

When we reconnect to the heart, we feel authentic emotions. In other words, we feel emotions for their own sake and without the need to justify, rationalise or temper them.

When we do not have good heart/mind connections we tend to have unauthentic emotions. This means we rationalise the inner feelings we have and relate them to our thinking. The result is that we may connect a feeling to a thought that will justify our need to vampirise.

A good example of this is blame. When we feel an uncomfortable emotion, we may seek out in our minds a reason, and decide that it is the "fault" of our partner/boss/friend etc. Rather than feeling the authentic, and perhaps uncomfortable emotion, the inner vampire unconsciously chooses to redirect the feeling into something that will serve its purposes, this could be anger aimed at another.

Unauthentic emotions are focussed on the outside; they are concerned with the effect of other people upon us. Authentic emotions, on the other hand, are genuine inner feelings that may not have any rational basis, but that are felt anyway. Feeling authentic emotions is ultimately satisfying, even when they are painful. This is particularly true for feelings of grief.

What does it mean to fly?

Flying means letting go of the need for approval from others. We do not need the approval of others to live a fulfilling and joyful life. Yet we prevent ourselves from pursuing what we truly want because of our fantasies about how other people view us. A perfect example is the gay man who married a women because he was afraid of what "people" might have said if he had "come out".

By behaving in this way we prevent ourselves from doing the things that would awaken joy and freedom in our lives. In our fantasies we assume that everyone is obsessed with the way we behave, that they are studying us.

It is true that if you make an exhibition of yourself people will probably look; usually more in admiration that scorn, for these are usually people who would so love to allow themselves to be free of approval, but feel they cannot. However being free is not about making yourself the centre of attention; it is about doing what you want to do, providing it does not harm another.

The Boomerang Effect:

A way of describing the Boomerang Effect would be to say, "we should always ensure the freedom we exercise does not imprison or abuse others". The Boomerang Effect is known to Pagans and Witches (a much maligned and misunderstood group of people), and is the one guiding principle in all of their work. Basically, it is a universal law that says whatever you project outwards you will get back three times over. If, therefore, you choose to do ill, you will receive your just rewards in bad luck and misfortune. If you do good, you will be rewarded by the power of nature and goodness and good fortune will befall upon you.

As Pagans and Witches believe this principle most heartily it is very unusual for you to find a so called "black" witch; this notion is a misnomer anyway to

 Fig 9.4 Angelic Voices Case Study: Jack and Amy

Amy's son, Jack, had been keen to learn how to dance for as long as either of them could remember. He was interested in pop music and tried to emulate the dances. Amy investigated modern dance classes but could find nothing locally that was appropriate, such as Jazz Dance for children.

One day, when Jack was nine years old, after watching him dance around the room, Amy suggested that perhaps he should try ballet . He said he would like that. A couple of days later he was dancing again, this time wearing a bird costume, and he asked Amy if she had found out about classes yet? "If you are that keen" Amy said jokingly, "you would dance around on the green in front of our house just as you are dancing now". "OK" Jack said and walked straight out the door and danced around on the green for the world to see, still in the bird costume. He came back inside and asked "Will you book up the classes for me now?"

Of course, Amy arranged the ballet lessons and Jack continued to take classes until he was fifteen years old. During this time he auditioned for the Central School of Ballet in London and for the National Youth Ballet. Although ballet has not become his career, it has given Jack a confidence and poise, the opportunity to perform and delight an audience, and an ability to move to music that will remain with him for life.

When Jack was twelve, he went to a Wayne Sleep Workshop, only to discover some of the girls in his class from school were also attending. Fearing he would be teased, Jack wanted to flee, "Brazen it out" Amy told him, don't let other people stop you from flying!" So he did. Wayne Sleep even invited the only three boys attending to have a private chat about their ballet—what a boon!

Back at school one of the girls approached him. Much to his surprise she asked if he did ballet, and Jack replied that yes, he did. She, and her friends had been interested, but never said another word about it.

"Always remember," Amy told him later, "that people want to be free to be themselves and admire those us who are confident enough to be. Be unapologetic about chasing your dream, and people will cheer you on, instead of booing and jeering".

Pagan society as it implies that people are either good or bad, and we all know that we are sometimes one and sometimes the other. But the important thing is this; we must intend good at all times, or we will pay the price, and in this lifetime, not in the "next"!

Therefore, when we allow ourselves to fly, we must never drag down or step on another in order to do so. It can be tempting to jump on someone else's back in order to launch ourselves into free flight. For example, we may use cruel or sarcastic humour, or believe that freedom of expression means we can shout and curse someone whose car has pulled out in front of us.

True freedom means freedom for all, otherwise it is only power over others. Just like Nazism promises freedom for the select few at the expense of other, innocent individuals, who happen to make good targets.

Interestingly, witches have always been known to fly, and have also been known for the "free lifestyle". The original witch was probably a wise woman who knew about healing and perhaps mind-altering herbs. Witches became synonymous with evil when a more male-dominated religion grew in prominence, female sexuality in particular, was considered dangerous. Now that we look upon enjoyment of sex as good and right, this attitude to witches seems a little ridiculous. In fact, the witch has come to represent a freedom of expression, in all senses. We can all learn to fly, and even those who fly on broomsticks may well be angels.

Exercise in learning to fly:

How often do you do what you want to do when you want to do it? This exercise will allow you to realise how often you suppress your natural instincts for pleasure.

Take a notepad, and note down every time that you would really like to do something but feel trapped by society (what "people" think is acceptable) or peers ("My friends would think I'm mad/stupid/foolish etc), family (I would never live it down/they would not love me anymore), work colleagues or boss (I would be considered disloyal/uncommitted/useless etc).

You may feel like bursting into song, or laughing out loud, or crying at a sad story, or telling someone you love their hairdo, or even just saying how you really feel about something or someone.

You do not need actually to do these things, but recognise what you feel and when you feel it. When you can do this you are half way towards taking flight.

Exercise in Mitigating the Boomerang Effect:

Following on from the above exercise, notice any of the freedoms you would like to express that may restrict another person's freedom, which may be unkind or even abusive.

Continue the above exercise, but this time find alternative responses to those that may be negative or unkind. In other words, focus on the things that you can do that will be truly freeing.

Exercise in Flying :

Now you are becoming aware of the things that will let you unleash your Angel of Freedom, choose one, starting with once each week, and note it in your notebook. Then increase this to two a week until you exercise freedom once everyday. To really fly these must always exist in the Sunshine of Joy, so use that as your rule of thumb.

Exercise in Flying—Visualisation:

Visualisation is an extremely powerful tool in creating change. If you want to learn how to fly then this tool can help you enormously.

First of all, imagine flying, really flying, as though you are soaring over the countryside, see the world from up in the air, fly over the top of all the problems and difficulties that you face in everyday life, see them from afar. Sometimes this in itself will change your perception sufficiently to help you to get a different and perhaps more meaningful perspective on things.

If you really put your heart and soul into this, as you carry out this exercise you will feel an amazing sense of freedom. You may feel exhilarated as you imagine the sensation of flying, as you climb higher or swoop low.

This feeling is a little scary, but it is also wonderful. After a while you will enjoy the experience so much that you will no longer feel scared, only fulfilled.

When you have managed to perfect flying, now you can try to fly in everyday situations. Imagine a situation that would create needy feelings, and then visualise those feelings as tethers that hold you to the ground. In your mind you can even label each tether, perhaps these are attachments to people or ideas or places. You have a sharp knife and you can cut through everyone of these tethers one at a time, and as you do you can thank it for keeping you in one piece, and then say goodbye forever as you now have your flying licence.

Then see that same situation but with you as a free thinking and freely behaving person, no encumbrances, nothing to hold you down, just flying in the face of all that had stopped you in the past. Once you feel it you will never go back to holding yourself down with attachments.

Trust Exercise:

Can you stand in front of a friend and fall backwards into their arms? This is a way of demonstrating trust, if you can do it, then you trust your friend with your safety.

Now think about the universe in the same way. When you fall backwards towards your friend, it is almost impossible for him or her *not* to catch you. It is instinctive to reach out and support our friends.

In the same way the universe will catch you when you let go, it is like resting on an infinite cushion, you feel safe and supported *because* there is no one to rely on, *not* in spite of it.

Accepting yourself:

How can you ever be abandoned? The feeling of being abandoned comes from neediness for others to administer to your needs. By whom are you being abandoned, and to what?

When we analyse the feeling of abandonment it is the feeling of being alone and without support. This is the very feeling we need to learn to love, because we are not unsupported.

Feeling abandoned is different from being alone. I have taken great pains to ensure that my children know what it feels like to be alone, and that they learn to like their own company.

When you spend time with yourself, and you like this person, you cannot feel abandoned or lonely. Remember that the process of growing into adulthood should be a process that allows us to let go of all the support structures that we

Fig 9.6 **Angelic Voices Case Study - Sanjay takes flight:**
I visited a pub because there was a beer festival and an Irish Folk Band playing The band was excellent and my partner desperately wanted to dance. She pleaded with me, but I was afraid of what people would think.

Then I thought about it more—I did not know these people very well, and I was not in the least bit interested in what they were doing, so why should they be interested in me? I realised that I was fantasising about their fascination with me and whether or not I danced. No one cared, they were interested in themselves, and whether or not they felt embarrassed.

I asked myself, "what do I think about the one or two people who are dancing?" My answer was "Good for them!" and perhaps I felt a little envy, as they were having such a good time!

It took courage, but I grabbed my partner, and we danced the night away. I am a useless, two left footed dancer, but no one seemed to notice or care. In fact, one acquaintance came up to me and said that she thought I looked as though I had really enjoyed myself.

She was right, I had a great time. I had a far better time than if I had stayed feet firmly on the ground. Flying is a little scary, but it is exhilarating and the risks are only an illusion.

believe we need, because when we do we realise that life is a lot easier, it is easy to have positive and rewarding relationships when we are not trying to hold onto them.

The best way of keeping a relationship going is to be self accepting. When we accept and value ourselves we become a valuable person and are therefore valued by others.

If you fear being abandoned it means you are low in self esteem and hungering after someone else's energy, because on the one hand you believe people do not (may/cannot) love you (vampires feel they are unlovable, if you remember), and on the other hand you feel that your life is less complete without the very relationship that is to abandon you.

We are never abandoned when we approve of and love ourselves. It is not possible to be abandoned when we are supported by the entirety of the universe, when all our energy requirements are provided when we need them.

 Fig 9.7 Angelic Voices **Case Study: Peter and Jim**

Peter, a trainer, was delighted when he eventually managed to capture a client, Jim, the manager of a local company whom he had been chasing for sometime. He enthusiastically designed a one year programme of training for the company.

Peter was ready to begin the programme when Jim asked if he could help him to deal with a pressing need. Peter slotted the new course in and changed his schedule. The response from the delegates was excellent, the training was considered exactly what they needed.

Jim then asked Peter to carry out some other "pressing" training, each course responding to specific issues that had arisen at work. Peter realised that he was "fire-fighting" on Jim's behalf, and felt dissatisfied about this because he was taking a "scatter gun" approach, and not following his original agreed plan.

After a while Jim contacted Peter and told him that the regular session they had booked for consolidating the learning would have to be cancelled this quarter. Peter agreed to amalgamate this session with the next one.

But by the next quarter the same thing happened. By this time the delegates were finding the learning too much, the subjects were muddled and they did not have time to implement their knowledge. Peter was disillusioned, he knew he could be helping the business to develop, but Jim seemed to be afraid to commit to anything he suggested.

Peter had numerous conversations with Jim, which always ended on a high note, as Jim committed himself to follow Peter's plan. Then Jim would change his mind again a few days later.

Peter made his decision. He amicably withdrew from the contract with Jim, which seemed to be a relief to them both.

From then on Peter changed his tack, he worked and spoke from the heart, he told his clients of his commitment and why he was planning his work as he did. Peter increased his client base within three months and had to take on two new trainers to cope with the workload.

Accepting yourself exercise:

When you feel rejected by someone else, make a point of being very accepting of yourself. This way you turn the attention away from "her and what she did" to "Me and how I feel".

When you feel rejected and /or abandoned recall times when you felt really in control and happy, confident and secure. Imagine that and visualise it as strongly as you can, so that the imagining becomes a meaningful experience.

When you have really felt that feeling, then let go and come back to now. Notice how you feel. You will bring those good feelings back with you and it will change the way you feel about now.

Remember lovingly to connect with all things. By doing this we mitigate completely any possibility of feeling rejected, because we cannot be rejected by the very universe of which we are a part. This would be like your hand rejecting your foot.

Summary:

When we let go of needing we become free; needing makes us prisoners.

We do not have to cling to things or people because the universe will always support us.

Authentic emotions are those that focus on the inside of ourselves, inauthentic ones are focussed on the outside.

When we use authentic emotions we take responsibility for how we feel, and do not blame another. We accept that uncomfortable feelings may have to be endured.

When we let go of needing we can be spontaneous and we are able to fly. This means we can fearlessly be ourselves, but we will only reach angelic heights if we work positively with the Boomerang effect.

MOSAIC Approach:	Examples:
Mission What do I want to achieve?	To awaken my ability to respond to my feelings at any time, so I can be myself.
Opportunity for improvement identified What areas in my life could do with improvement and change?	To let go of old hurts that make me feel needy or fear being abandoned.
Skills and abilities are assessed. What am I able to do, what will require practice?	I am capable of saying what I need but I will have to practice not blaming.
Atmosphere is assessed What are things like around me? How supportive are family/friends/colleagues?	I have the greatest difficulty at work, and the atmosphere here is not supportive, so I will ensure I "bring my support team with me to work" such as having a photo on my desk, or meeting friends at lunchtime.
Impact of changes are considered Will there be problems, if so what are they likely to be and can I deal with them?	My boss may misunderstand if I behave as though I do not *need* my job, so I will have to ensure this is replaced with positive enthusiasm and genuine commitment.
Catalyst: What can I do to speed changes into place? What will work as a catalyst for me?	Carry out the "Flying Exercises" and remembering to imagine myself flying over the roof tops, free!

"Change Thinking" Assignments ✓

I allow myself to soar by letting go of the need for approval from others.	
I now take opportunities everyday to be me without fearing rejection, I no longer concern myself with what others will think.	
Waking Mantra:	
I am the real me, flying through life.	

"Take Action" Assignments ✓

Notice where you set "rules" for friends and then let those rules go.	
Stop thinking, thinking, thinking and begin feeling.	
Practice trusting—you do not need to hold on in order to survive, you will not fall.	
Stop taking draconian measures every time someone says or does something that upsets you. Make a point of forgiving and not "forgiving on condition" that they apologise and never do it again!	
When you notice that you feel a sense of abandonment or rejection by someone, make a point of being very accepting of yourself.	
Stop trying to put other people right. When you feel people have "done you wrong" look inside and fix yourself!	

Chapter 10

Step 4- The Angel of Courage

Discover:
How to antidote the Charismatic Vampire
How to shine

How to Antidote the Charismatic Vampire:

The Charismatic Vampire likes to live in the spotlight. When we commit it to the purifying flames it can be reborn just as the phoenix is reborn, without all the clutter and baggage of the past.

Shining:

The Charismatic Vampire is the star, or the seducer. It likes to bask in reflected glory, but in fact, takes the shine off any achievement. The Charismatic Vampire represents the fascination we have with celebrity. Whether these are on the TV, film, media, or in our own small circle of friends and acquaintances. People will gather round the celebrity, and so the Charismatic Vampire makes itself into a celebrity, by stealing from others, by attaching itself to "the right" people, by being the life and soul of the party.

They will do anything to maintain that position, because they so desperately need to be at the centre of things. If the Charismatic Vampire is unseen, it assumes it is invisible, and invisibility is what it fears most.

What is the inner Charismatic Vampire?

Our Charismatic Vampire comes to light when we try to be the centre of attention, or bask in reflected glory, such as the parent who takes responsibility for his child's excellent examination results.

In both cases we are putting ourselves into the spotlight, showing off. We can allow our own brilliance to shine forth, but when we are vampires we do not see this as worthy. We believe it is insignificant or we are afraid that it will not be appreciated; our true self is not of value to the world.

False Teaming:

Charismatic Vampires often use extremely subtle methods for trapping a victim. For example, false teaming. This involves drawing you into their world, or bringing themselves into your world, uninvited. This can be done in such a way that you do not notice, although you may feel uncomfortable.

When this vampire wants to draw you into its world when talking about *its* problem it will say things like "We really must sort this problem out, mustn't we". Or if it wants to draw itself into your world when talking about *your* situation, which may be something you can cope with on your own, it may say "Lets see what we can do about this."

Causing the Charismatic Vampire to rise in others:

You may experience seeing only the light and not the dark in a person. This may be a mentor that was very good at their job and whom you admired, it may be an attractive lover, in any case we can sometimes cause their Charismatic Vampire to rise from grave

How do we antidote the Charismatic Vampire within?

Burning can destroy vampires. And this Vampire must be burned until it leaves no more than the ashes of its former self, because from the ashes can rise the phoenix, the fire bird.

The phoenix, a bird of incredible beauty, is born from the flames. The destruction of the fire is the only thing that will allow this creature to come forth into the world, anew and in its youthful prime.

When we hold onto our Charismatic Vampire we are holding onto the clutter in our lives. The old stuff we have carried around for years, that has no value other than to reinforce our view that we cannot be truly ourselves in case we are not likeable.

The Bag Lady:

Under the top hat and tails of this entertaining and fascinating creature, our Charismatic Vampire, is a bag lady. The bag lady holds onto everything, and most of it is rubbish, a good proportion is revolting, and when the bags are opened the stench is likely to hit you in the face. It is the smell of rank and putrid old fears, failures and expectations.

The Charismatic Vampire will endeavour to cover this disgusting side with a show of behaviours that create the impression of a confident person, who is "in control", or simply someone fascinating, whose views or ideas or preferences will attract you.

The bag lady is covered in the dirt and grime from relationships where there was plenty of mud slinging. Oh yes, this vampire will not quit a relationship without making sure the other party feels like rubbish, or dirt, or pointless.

Charismatic Vampires may appear beautiful, but they can be violent in the way they use their tongue; sometimes even physically threatening or violent. It is so difficult for the partner of a Charismatic Vampire to be believed by others when she tells them of her brutalising Charismatic Vampire of a husband. It cannot be so, people think, he is *so* charming.

No matter what happens, the Charismatic Vampire will hold onto the belief that it is right, it will stay on the pedestal and throw everybody else off, if necessary; anything than admit to being wrong.

People involved with Charismatic Vampires will notice that the façade can slip after a while, and when this happens it causes a stink; those smelly bags of yesterday's clutter reek. The partner may love the Vampire, but find it difficult to love the bag lady, and so the partner wills the Vampire to continue using the vampiric behaviours, and continues to be a victim of those.

This is so often the case with beaten wives. They are addicted to vampirism, often the brutaliser concerned will be using his Charismatic Vampire in remaining attractive on the outside.

There is an alternative, we can commit Vampire and Bag Lady to the flames and rise as phoenix, reborn and renewed.

How to shine

When we can let go of the limitations that cause us to use vampiric behaviours we can shine. This means first finding out what our brilliance is and then having the courage to be wonderful.

Burning Rubbish:
The best way to rid the bag lady of her hideous baggage is to allow her willingly to incinerate it. She burns it so that the infections of the years can be purified in the flames. The Charismatic Vampire within us must do the same. We must allow ourselves to let go of the baggage we are secretly carrying, and learn to have the courage to be our true selves.

The Purifying Flames:
The flames represent our need to strip away the baggage of our past, and allow our self to get back to the true person beneath. This "true" person is still there, and has always been there, and yet the messages we have received from others,

the experiences we have had on our life's journey and the expectations we pour upon ourselves and others have obscured our true self.

Fire helps us to clear ourselves of clutter. It is usual for us to create a big bonfire of all the things we want to destroy from our lives, whether it is garden waste, old papers or the remnants of a relationship that is over.

Clutter impedes progress; like the bag lady, it is difficult to travel unless you travel light. A Vampire never travels light. It always takes its coffin, heavy with the earth of its homeland. It always takes its household. A Vampire loves clutter; its house is a gothic warehouse, full of memories, each covered in a veil of cobwebs and dust. And what is dust but the dead skin of the living? What an interesting and appropriate shroud to cover the photographs and treasures of the past, but the dead skin of those who have gone before, as though this will keep them alive. No, instead it makes us cough and splutter, it gets in our eyes and dulls the beauty of old memories.

Beneath the vampire is the egg of the phoenix. An egg is only potential, it is not properly formed until it is hatched, and this egg carried a huge potential.

Case Study—Hijacking Her Life:

As work colleagues, Gillian and Jane got on very well. Jane felt Gillian was a genuine person, one of energy and vibrancy, and one she would like to have as a friend as well as a colleague, the feeling seemed to be mutual.

On one occasion Jane told Gillian about a "crazy time" when she and her boyfriend had been visiting the grounds of a Castle and, out of the blue, Jane said how she had felt a great desire to sing at the top of her voice (Jane was very good at allowing her Angel of Freedom full rein). However, her boyfriend, out of fun, was determined to prevent her, and so they had a manic time jumping onto park benches with Jane singing as much as she could before her boyfriend could stop her with a kiss.

Jane enjoyed telling the story to Gillian, who seemed to think it extremely funny. It was some time later that the two of them were sitting with a group of work colleagues all laughing and sharing stories when Jane brought up how she loved to sing at any chance. Gillian then told the group about an occasion when *she* had embarrassed *her* boyfriend by singing in public jumping up on park benches at the grounds of a Castle. Jane innocently piped up that she too had done this when out with *her* boyfriend.

Then the penny dropped. Jane came to a realisation that Gillian was telling the group *her* story. Gillian had hijacked it! Jane's reaction was to feel embarrassed on Gillian's behalf, and rather than continue with her own anecdote, she cut it short. Gillian knew she had been caught out but she never said a word about this to Jane.

Jane did not try to command the spotlight from Gillian, and in resisting this she realised that she had a tendency to play the Charismatic Vampire herself. She realised that she could have the courage to be herself without requiring others to be her essential audience.

It carries the firebird, the bird that can rise from the flames and glow, shining out its beauty and magnificence.

There is only one way to hatch a phoenix egg. It has to be placed in the fire, the very flames that consume everything, will be the ones that bring forth the phoenix. If ever a vampire needed to die in order to be reborn, it is this one.

Becoming the Phoenix:

The Angel of Courage can come in the guise of the phoenix, which represents re-birth, and for us it means finding our true inner value. The phoenix is within us all, and yet we try very hard to prevent it from hatching. We fear the flames. It is scary to have to let go of all the old wounds and beliefs that have served to keep us on that pedestal. The trouble is, we feel so vulnerable up there, and we have to expend and gain enormous amounts of energy just to remain there.

The difference between shining and showing off:

When we show off we like to have the spotlight pointing directly at ourselves. We are in the light, and this means that everyone else is in the dark. The others, who are a part of our performance, are in the shadows, perhaps "back stage" or perhaps just out of the limelight. Everyone else is part of the audience, and we are in no doubt about who is centre stage.

When we are showing off we take the full credit, we do not give any recognition to those who have supported or helped us. We certainly try hard to ensure that anyone who has been a part of our success is forgotten, in case they should step into the spotlight and push us out.

When we are showing off, we need the light to be pointed on us. It is up to others to point the spotlight in our direction, and if they move the light off us and onto someone else, we push ourselves back into the limelight to ensure we are still centre stage.

When we awaken the Angel of Courage and shine we do not need a spotlight. We do not need an audience, and we do not deny the presence of others or their contribution. When we shine we see our success as everyone's success. We are one with them and they with us.

When we shine we automatically give permission to others to shine, and we enjoy their moments as much as our own, because we feel it, we connect with everyone, and so we do not feel jealous of their impact, nor need to hi-jack it.

The shining light comes from within and shines upon everyone. It lights up people's faces, and they feel empowered to let their own light shine.

Hi-jacking:

Charismatic Vampires appear to respect people, but they do not. It is only when we can truly respect ourselves that we can offer others their rightful respect. Hi-jacking is an example of how the Charismatic Vampire in us fails to respect itself and others. The Vampire will shamelessly take the idea from another and claim ownership. This happens in the workplace frequently, when the insecure Charismatic Vampire boss takes the ideas from a subordinate without giving credit for them.

The Native American view of ownership is that we belong to the earth, rather than the earth belonging to us. How true this is! We are here for a short time, but the earth has been here since the beginning. Perhaps all ideas belong to us all, and not to one person. Therefore, perhaps we should give credit to people for bringing the idea to the table without feeling that it diminishes our power if we do not claim it as our own.

Hatching the Phoenix—Exercise:

This exercise allows you to awaken your Angel of Courage and experience your potential. Start by noting down all the things at which you are brilliant.

You should get a list of at least 10 things within 3 minutes. If not, continue with the following exercise, preferably, in pairs, with one partner guiding the other through the process. Otherwise, work alone by reading each section at a time, and then taking the time to think.

This exercise will help you to realise that you have a wealth of possibilities still within you. If you can imagine what it would be like to be a success, then you can make that feeling come into your life now, in reality. The exercise will help you to find an inner experience that you can draw upon to allow you to feel confident and courageous about taking positive steps into your future.

Fig 10.1 **Shining Forth Your Brilliance**			
Note at least 10 things at which you are brilliant. It can be anything, but it must be something at which you are brilliant and not simply "very good". If you cannot think of 10 different things, go through the Phoenix Hatching Exercise first.			
1		6	
2		7	
3		8	
4		9	
5		10	

Taking things out of the bags:

The bag lady in us needs to take things out of the bags in order to cast them into the flames, in order to do this we must rise above the earthly fear of losing our possessions and awaken our Angel, as it takes considerable courage to face our clutter and baggage and discard it forever.

We are many layered, like the layers on an onion, and we need to peel these away one at a time. This onion can be seen in fig. 10.2.

10.1i Hatching the Phoenix
1 Close your eyes and imagine that you are going back in time...you are getting younger and younger and now you are in your teens, you are now ten years old, now 9,8,7,6,5,4,3,2,1 year old. And now you are only just born.
2 Imagine yourself as a tiny baby. You have the world of possibility before you. You have infinite potential. Imagine yourself looking down at you as a baby. Imagine thinking, I wonder what this baby could be? The world of possibility is before her/him. S/he could be anything s/he chooses.
3 Now imagine what you would truly like to be in your life. When you can think of something you would like to be, but have never been able to pursue, project forward 25 years. Do not proceed until you have read the next bit, as this is important. **It is essential that when you do this you skip over all the experiences that you have had in your life, all the messages you have received.** In other words, you are **not** reliving those times, you are re-inventing them. You are moving from being a baby to being an adult, without having to experience any of the reality that took from there to here. You must **not** return to your youth as it was. Instead you will return to your youth without any baggage, no memories, nothing except your potential.
4 What would you really like to have achieved by the time you were, say, 25 years old? This is your chance to live it, to see what it would be like. So jump forward in time and be that 25 year old, remembering you are going from being a baby (with all your potential) to being a 25 year old in one step, with nothing in between.
5 Now you are perhaps 25 years old and doing the job you wanted to do, but you have skipped all the experiences and messages in your life, you have arrived at 25 directly from being a baby, and you still have your endless possibilities intact.
6 Describe your life in detail—Such as your job; what do you see, what do you hear and what do you feel? Do not just focus on the idealised image, describe the day to day experience, what is it really like? Is it as ideal as you imagined now you are experiencing doing the actual work? Decide if you like this job. If not go back to being a baby again and skip to step 9. (see fig 10.1ii)

10.1 ii Hatching The Phoenix Continued
7   If you do like this job ensure that you really get a sense of what you feel—such as fulfilled. Remember this feeling. You can come back to this anytime you want to. It is a little refuge that will remind you of what it feels like to be fulfilled or satisfied, or whatever other positive feelings you felt.
8   Now move ahead 10 years and see what life is like then. Again describe it in detail. What has happened? What has changed? What do you like about it? Do you still like the job? If you want to you can move on a further 10 years—it doesn't matter if this is into the future or not. How do you feel? Remember any good feelings, such as confidence.
9   When you have fully experienced this return to "being a baby", in other words, go back to that feeling of being new in the world with limitless possibilities ahead of you, and with nothing that may undermine this sense that anything is possible or that greatness is probable.
10   Now, move forward in time to the present, but this time skip all your experiences, so that you arrive back in the present with your potential and limitless possibilities intact. Now, knowing you have arrived with all the beliefs and possibilities you had as a baby, make a note of all the things you are brilliant at. Go back to the questionnaire (fig 10.1). Free yourself, enjoy shining because it feels wonderful and you have the right to enjoy this and value yourself.

How we formed:
Peeling back the onion 1 - Our Natal or Birth Potential:
Natal refers to birth, so this is the potential we are all born with. This is at the centre of the onion. It is the truth of who we are and what we could achieve, untainted by experiences and messages received through life. This is the egg of the phoenix. If we can allow the flames to consume each of the outer layers we can hatch this potential and come into our brilliance.

Peeling back the onion 2 -Our Beliefs:
Close to the inner self is our "beliefs". These are what we believe about life, ourselves etc. In other words, we quickly begin to create clear ideas about who we are as children, and these form a basis for who we are as adults. As we grow we may alter and develop our "beliefs", they become what we perceive to be true, and not necessarily what is reality. A belief we may hold dear is honesty, for example, we may believe that honesty is always right.

Peeling back the onion 3 -Our Rules:
In order to live within these beliefs we have invented for ourselves, we create a number of rules. These help to ensure that we maintain these beliefs. In other words, our rules state clear ways in which we should behave. For instance, if I believe myself to be kind, I will set up a rule that says that I must always be kind to others. This can be a problem if I also have a rule that states that I should be honest, because sometimes the truth is painful.

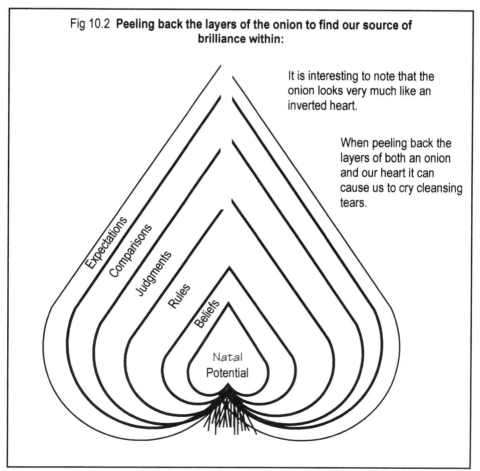

Fig 10.2 **Peeling back the layers of the onion to find our source of brilliance within:**

It is interesting to note that the onion looks very much like an inverted heart.

When peeling back the layers of both an onion and our heart it can cause us to cry cleansing tears.

Expectations
Comparisons
Judgments
Rules
Beliefs
Natal Potential

Peeling back the onion 4 -Judgements we make:

The next layer is our judgements of ourselves, or how we assess ourselves and judge ourselves to be either "right or wrong". When we have meted out judgement we may then take action for or against ourselves. If we perceive ourselves to be "wrong" then we may berate or even punish ourselves.

Peeling back the onion 5 -Comparisons we make:

Further out from our judgement of ourselves, is comparison we make between ourselves and others; assessing ourselves in relation to other people, and others in relation to ourselves. This may mean that we look more or less kindly upon others depending upon how we judge them in comparison to our rules and ourselves. It is from here that we feel vindicated in criticising others.

After we make comparisons with others we then take action, which may be either for or against ourselves or others.

For example, we may criticise the way someone looks or dresses, mockingly or even with disdain, because we consider our own dress sense superior, as it conforms to *our* rules about how people should be.

Peeling back the onion 6 -Expectations we have:

Our expectations are the outside layer. This is the "surface" manifestation of our rules, judgements and comparisons. As expectations are based upon a complex interaction between our rules, judgements and comparisons we may set ourselves up with expectations that inhibit freedom of expression or flexibility of action in life. In order to get to the core of the onion we need to peel back the layers one at a time, starting with the outermost.

Committing to the purifying flames:

Look at the example that relates to driving in fig. 10.3. Use this as a framework for challenging your own thinking so that the Angel of Courage can shine forth. In other words, by getting to the bottom of your beliefs, you can re-evaluate them and lose those that no longer serve you, or you can redefine them. In this way you can be kinder to yourself instead of judgmental.

Michael—The Angel of Courage:

The Archangel Michael, leader and commander in chief of all the archangels and angels, with a sword in hand, is at the ready to overcome the darkness with light. He is often depicted holding a set of scales in his hand, and in this form he makes the astrological symbol of Libra, the last day of Libra being Michaelmas (29th September).

Fig 10.3 **Committing to the Flames 1 :** Unpacking the baggage and releasing the clutter that keeps the Inner Charismatic Vampire in business.		
Layers of the self	**Questions to ask ourselves in order to unpack the limiting clutter.**	**Example: Woman driver who has recently had a car accident.**
Expectations	What are the kinds of expectations that people have in life?	I expect to be able to get into my car and drive without any problems. I expect that getting from A to B should be easy and quick. (This may not be a realistic expectation—because they *are* frequently unrealistic)
Comparisons	How do the expectations that you have identified result in comparisons?	I consider myself to be a poor driver as I have had a previous accident. (My skill level tends to be exaggerated to either better than or worse than most others, but in reality I don't know with whom I am comparing myself. It is just an idea in my mind.)
Judgement	How do we determine whether we consider ourselves right or wrong?	I have had an accident just recently. This was not my fault, but it affects the way I judge myself. This is now a part of the messages and experiences I have had that lead me to think that I am a bad driver. Regardless of fault, things are not as I expected and compared with my false idea of how others behave on the roads, I I judge myself to be wrong.
Rules	How must you behave?	My rules are : "I must always drive perfectly and therefore never have an accident."
Beliefs	What do we believe about life and/or ourselves?	My belief is "As I have had an accident I am a bad driver regardless of fault. Also, as I am a woman who has had an accident, I am confirming the established view that women are poor drivers, and perhaps I am buying into a myth."
Natal Potential	What is the real truth?	Now I can question the above: Are all women bad drivers? Does having an accident make you a bad driver? The key thing is that regardless of whether it is your fault or not, it doesn't necessarily make you a bad driver.
Hatching the Phoenix	Challenge yourself with a different scenario in order to get to the real truth and unlock your natal potential.	My alternative scenario may be "If I slip up when walking down the street, does this make me a bad walker?" Therefore, one accident does not make me a bad driver; it just makes me someone who has had an "accident".

When we awaken the archangel Michael we are able to find our inner light, we are able to shine out our brilliance, we realise our dreams. Our relationships become harmonious, as Michael maintains a balance between the Virgin (Virgo) and the Dragon (Scorpio). He steers a path of truth and light, knowing himself, and, therefore being able to choose his pathway wisely.

When we awaken this angel, we let go of the spotlight, have the courage of our convictions and maintain the balance. Michael carries the scales of justice and the sword of truth. When we awaken this angel we can become true leaders, and an inspiration to others. In order to do this we need to remember the words of Nietzsche, "He who does not command himself will be commanded."

Becoming a Leader:

The mistake the Charismatic vampire makes is in thinking that being a leader means being at the front. In fact, being a leader can mean listening as much as talking, allowing others to shine in their roles, rather than feeling we have to have all the glory, and knowing that it is the whole team who should take the credit for the team's success.

The Charismatic Vampire believes that as a leader it is above or better than the team, therefore it does not expect to have to work the same hours or suffer the same irritations. Its view is that Leadership carries privilege. In fact leadership carries responsibility, and what is that other than the ability to respond.

Being Responsible—Our ability to respond:

Responsibility is only a burden to carry when we do not connect with it and with the people around us to whom or for whom we are responsible. Then we lose our energy and become exhausted by it.

Whenever we respond by combining our natal potential (our belief in our inner infinite abilities) with the reality of our current resources, whether they be things or places or people, we are being responsible. When we do this it is an energising experience. We become courageous beings, radiating our light, shining out our inner potential and rising to every challenge.

How we can create Charismatic Vampires in our children:

Childcare practices have changed over the century. The Truby-King philosophy has long since been usurped; his approach was along the lines of "feed your baby four hourly only and otherwise let him cry or he will become spoilt".

Then when Rene Spitz discovered that institutionalised babies were dying from lack of love and cuddles, attitudes began to alter.

Now we have moved on. We appreciate the need to show love and appreciation. We realise that children need to feel secure in love, and that now many parents do not find it too difficult to say, "I love you".

Even those parents that were not used to saying this to their children, who were not brought up hearing it said to them, are showing that they can say "I love you" in the things they do. We can never spoil a child with love, we can never love anyone too much. But we can become confused about the line between showing love and gaining love.

When we perpetually put our children into the spotlight and allow them to experience that feeling of being central, when we let them show off, we allow the vampire to rise. They quickly discover the instant fix that they can get from being seen, being appreciated for what they can do. Our children may never learn humility, and may feel that they must spend the rest of their lives living up to the position they occupy on the golden pedestal.

When they are on this pedestal we see perfection in them, and they have to hide anything that is going to be perceived as unsavoury. For example, the child that realises that he is gay, and yet cannot tell his father because he feels his father will be disappointed at best and insulted and disgusted at worst. This child is upon the pedestal his parents created for him, and now his Charismatic Vampire will provide the energy he needs, rather than allowing and trusting love to flow freely.

Any parent that truly loves his or her child unconditionally will see every aspect of that child, as he or she grows into an adult, as loveable. The gay child is just a child, the same child before the announcement of his or her sexuality as after.

The responsibility of "Wow":

Being put upon a pedestal can begin early. Many parents do this by over-using the word "Wow!" in response to anything and everything their child says. Wow has become the stock answer to a child. Children's Television presenters are amongst the worst culprits; when asked on a live phone-in, "What are you going to do today?" by a TV presenter a child may give the response "I'm going shopping" to which the presenter will answer, "Wow!" No, it is not "Wow", it may be pleasant, or interesting or fun, but no, definitely not "Wow".

Whatever the quality of work our children show us we will frequently answer "Wow", whatever news they give us; "Wow". We are making their lives one dimensional, everything is FANTASTIC, or AMAZING, and nothing is simple and quiet and sufficient.

There is nowhere to go from "Wow", there is nothing better, unless we "Double Wow", or "Wowsy Wow" but now we are just getting silly. Besides which, wow is not even a real word.

An expression that comes to mind is "damned by faint praise"; *faint* praise being as bad, if not worse, than none at all. I remember my Grandmother replying to my sister's enquiry as to whether she liked her Christmas gift with "most acceptable, dear"; hmm ... there is some faint praise for you.

In the case of wow it is more a matter of damned by far too much over-the-top praise, because it becomes completely meaningless to the recipient, for example, if I am used to wow meaning, that's OK, then when I get anything less I feel a failure.

In our attempt to enable our children to feel secure and loved, we have confused conditional love with unconditional love. Instead of saying "That piece of work was not your best, and I love you just as much!" we are giving a different message, we are saying our approval for what the children *do* is linked with our unconditional love.

Unconditional love is unconditional and should never be confused with anything else. Approval should be unconditional for the person. We can dislike what they say or do, we can disagree with their approach or attitude, but in the end, if we still love and approve of our children as people, then we will ensure they remain secure and loved and loveable.

Fig 10.4 **Giving Feedback**		
Giving Feedback	Example: Child Negative Feedback	Example: Adult Positive Feedback
Tell him/her what it was that s/he did	You went over to your friends house without telling me where you were going.	You tidied the whole house up, and it was in such a mess.
Tell him/her how you felt about what s/he did (conditional)	I felt worried when I couldn't find you and really disappointed in you when I knew where you were.	I felt so relieved it felt as though a huge weight had been lifted from my shoulders.
Share a moment of silence while you connect and share feelings	(Silently standing to allow the feelings to wash over the child)	(Silently standing, smiling to allow the good feelings to wash over the adult)
Tell him/her that you love him/her (unconditional)	You are usually so thoughtful about these things. I love you so much, come here, lets have a hug.	I love you.

Communicating Satisfaction and Dissatisfaction:

In order to avoid confusion between conditional and unconditional love we use this simple method for giving feedback. It works as well with adults as it does with children (See Fig 10.4).

1. Tell him/her what it was that s/he did
2. Tell him/her how you felt about what s/he did (conditional)
3. Share a moment of silence while you connect and share feelings
4. Tell him/her that you love him/her (unconditional)

If you are using this method to give feedback to people at work for example, you may wish to alter step 4 and tell him/her how you feel about him or her in less intimate ways, such as "I feel honoured to work with you", "I am proud to be your friend" etc.

It makes no difference whether you use this method for giving positive or negative feedback, providing in both cases you include step 4, so that recipient feels O.K. as a person, and does not feel attacked.

Case study— Kuldip:

Kuldip was a bright and able girl of 18 years old, she had passed 10 G.C.S.E. subjects at ordinary level and was taking her Advanced level examinations that summer. She knew she was intelligent and capable, and that great things were expected of her. Her parents were supportive and told her not to worry, she would pass with flying colours.

All her life her parents had supported the view that she was a brilliant child, and now she wanted to study medicine, knowing that she had to get the highest possible grades.

The day before her first examination she went missing, and after a day and night of sheer misery and worry for her parents, she was found and brought back home.

Her parents were confused by the strange behaviour, she had never been unreliable before. Kuldip said that she had only known herself as a bright girl, and, in the run up to the exams had lost sight of anything else. If she had failed in her examinations she would no longer have any identity and her whole life would be ruined as she would be unable to follow her carefully mapped out career.

Kuldip needed time to discover that she was valuable as a human being, not just as a brain. She needed to learn to trust herself, her parents and life. When she decided to go with the flow, she went back to school, took her exams and did not get the high grades she needed. However, she also decided that she could wait to decide upon her future career, that she had her whole life in front of her, and sought balance rather than accolades.

Interestingly, she was terrified to tell her parents that she no longer wanted to be a Doctor, because she felt they would be disappointed. In fact, they were relieved that they were at last beginning to understand her better, and realised that they had not seen how their little girl had changed as she had grown. Now they are enjoying getting to know Kuldip, the young adult.

Learning to be alone:

Children who are likely to become Vampires will be overly demanding. They will expect their parents to provide everything for them, to entertain, to transport, to cook, to clean and tidy after them. They will not like to spend moments quietly in their own company.

Until we are able to spend moments alone and like being with ourselves we will continually seek out people from whom we can gain that sense of approval. We will want to be in someone's spotlight.

When as adults and children we can learn how to be happy in the empty moments, in the quiet and lonely times, then we can discover that we can be our own best companion. We must do this in order to slough off the baggage of the past and commit it to the flames. Leaping into the metaphorical fire is painful, but necessary. It can only be done alone.

Giving too much and causing the vampire to rise in children:

If we give our children too much, so that they have everything now, they will need thrills later of bigger kinds. We can never spoil children with too much love, but we can with too much attention and too many things.

For example, when we lavish attention on children so that we allow them to interrupt us when we are speaking to others, they will not respect us as people. This is a bad model, as models teach our children much more than what we tell them. It teaches them to have little respect for themselves, as we appear to have little for ourselves.

If we always subordinate our own wishes to our children we are demonstrating our lack of importance as people and our servitude as parents. Do we want our children to grow up to be servants to their children? Or to be fulfilled people who lovingly give themselves to the role of parent?

Whether you choose to devote yourself to your children's upbringing by being at home with them, or whether you find someone trusted to be there while you work, it makes no difference to this concept. It is not a matter of whether these choices are right or wrong. Only the parent and the child can know this. Children may grow up secure and happy when they have brought up by parents who work and those who do not. Furthermore, it is not the child minder that brings up the child. Yes, she has an influence, but it is the parents who have the ultimate bond, mother and father. And this bond is usually created from birth, but not always. Sometimes when a child is adopted it can be created later in life. But it is a bond that is fundamental to the child's present and future life.

Gender and sex is also irrelevant in parents, although I believe that both

160

parents' energy is ideally necessary even if the child has two mothers or two fathers in the case of stepchildren or gay partners.

Giving should be from the heart, and not measured in toys, pocket money, the latest fad or fashion. This simply puts them back onto that pedestal. When children accept the simple stuff, without the trappings and accessories of today, we are well on the way to allowing them to shine.

Giving too much and causing the vampire to rise in adults:

The same is true of adults. When we lavish ourselves upon our partners we can cause their vampires to rise from the grave. They need us and then blame us when things do not work out. We cannot control life for others, but we can love them and allow them to live for themselves.

 Angelic Voices Case Study—Simple Stuff:
We took our seven year old for a walk in Ashdown Forest, which is near where we live. His response was "Hooray!" He was thrilled to find a stick that was particularly fine, and take it home with him. Afterwards, he said thank you to us for taking him to such a wonderful place. I felt this was a success for the simple stuff!

The courage to love the whole person:

We need to have the courage to love every aspect of the individual, such as the anger within the child, because this is the flip side of the passion. Let us not suppress the person, as children will need to experience the range of emotions before they can understand how to use them appropriately. Let us continue to guide them, but without returning to our own baggage. Let us allow our children to awaken their Angel of Courage, this may mean that we have to let go and allow them to stand on their own two feet. It means we have to have the courage to allow them to "fail".

If we can accept that failure is simply a judgement we make according to the rules, comparisons and expectations we have formulated, then we can allow our children to revel in the experiences and come out stronger people.

Angelic Voices Tim and Phil—Dare to Lose to Win:

Tim had been dating his boyfriend for a year, and felt no closer to a permanent relationship. He was bothered by the fact that Phil wanted to maintain his independence by having his own flat and group of friends. Phil was gregarious and loved to socialise, whereas Tim liked the quiet things in life, enjoyed the countryside and reading in his garden at any chance he could get.

Tim had tried to be the "party animal" that Phil appeared to enjoy being with, and it was wearing him down. He felt more and more like he was not being true to himself and that this was affecting their relationship, causing him to snap at Phil quite frequently when Phil wanted to be "freer" and Tim felt unvalued and annoyed by this. They would argue and Phil would walk out and slam the door. Sometimes they would not see each other for a week, and Tim was convinced that when this happened Phil was seeing other men.

The situation was making Tim so miserable that Phil began to wonder what it was that brought them together in the first place.

Tim made a decision. Things could not get any worse as they were so he decided to take action. To begin with Tim stopped berating Phil for seeing his friends, in fact he encouraged him to go out and have fun, explaining that he was really not into this kind of socialising, but that he didn't begrudge Phil enjoying himself. Tim then invited Phil round for a special occasion and cooked him his favourite meal and then told him that he had decided to move to the country. He had found a beautiful cottage with a lovely garden. He explained to Phil that he was not at home in the urban gay scene, although he was not against coming back to town regularly; he really wanted a quiet life with the partner he loved. He told Phil how he envisaged life in the country to be and that he wanted Phil to come with him.

Phil's reaction was mixed. He was glad to hear Tim's honesty, but was still not convinced that they were able to make a go of the relationship. A move like this would be a big undertaking for him. However, Tim did not try to convince Phil, he simply asserted that he would love them to be life partners and that he believed they could make it work.

Tim moved to his cottage and did feel lonely to begin with, but he made an effort not to use this as an opportunity to make Phil feel guilty when he came to see him. On the contrary, he showed him all the joys of country living.

Phil began by spending a weekend or two with Tim and then stopped visiting.

Tim made friends of his own, he was completely accepted in the small community, his initial fears being replaced by respect and kindness. He was urged to join in with village events, and entered his garden produce into the village show. Tim began to shine, he felt at home here, he was able to pursue his career as a teacher locally, and everyday felt like a new adventure. He came to a realisation that he no longer needed Phil in his life.

Then, an extraordinary thing happened. Phil visited one weekend and told Tim that he wanted them to live together, that he wanted to move out to the country, that the urban scene was boring him, and that he found too many of his "friends" were fickle. He realised that Tim's life had changed and that he may not want him back, but Phil claimed he was ready to make a commitment.

Did Tim still want Phil? This was the question Tim now asked himself, but the truth was that they were really destined for each other and Phil settled into the lifestyle. Now they have been together for ten years. Phil still commutes three times a week to work, and spends the other days working at home. Phil realises that by seeing Tim shine he too can shine, and be himself.

Phil laid his Charismatic Vampire to rest and found the love that both he and Tim wanted, but no longer "needed".

Dare to lose to win:
This principle is true in all walks of life. The foremost football coaches in the world now focus their attention, not simply on practising skill, but also in mental attitude. The players that are at a world class standard are the players who can "dare to lose to win".

When we feel nervous about our ability we stop behaving automatically and our movements become stilted and childlike. We cannot function well and we fail. This is why great football players can make a complete mess of a simple thing like taking a penalty when the match depends on it.

When the player gets into "the zone" as it is called, they visualise and ensure that they are able to work from the unconscious part of the brain, by telling themselves "I can do this", and by being prepared to risk that it may not work.

As soon as we let go of the importance of an event, trust ourselves and allow ourselves to risk losing, our unconscious brain kicks in, and we become highly competent.

In relationships we sometimes need to dare to lose to win. We need to trust our partners, colleagues and friends, and we need to know that we must allow ourselves to be true to ourselves, we must let the real person shine forth and not be afraid that this may cause failure in that relationship. Fear of losing makes us behave in a stilted and unnatural way; we become protective and come across as something we are not. This prevents us from shining.

Case Study Dare to Lose to Win:
I had always believed that I was non-competitive. I believed that if I were to play a game of tennis I would lose, not because I had no skill, but because I had no desire to win. However, in a team game or when playing doubles I worked hard, because I would not want to let down the team or my partner.

One day a friend told me that my assertion that I was "non-competitive" showed that I was, in fact, extremely competitive. "What do you mean?" I asked, thinking this was completely ridiculous. "You are so competitive that you would rather not compete than lose", she told me. Ouch! How true it was. I had to win or I would not play.

So I determined to change, and the next time I played tennis I put heart and soul into it, I visualised and ace for every serve, and I ran for every ball. I lost, but I lost with dignity, because I put up a good fight!

This experience reminded me of a tennis tournament I had entered as a child. I went with my Girl Guide Company, because I would volunteer for everything that was going. When we arrived we found our competitors were from tennis clubs, and they all were very skilful. Naturally every one of us lost. I believe that the experience underlined the fact that I would not succeed at everything I attempted, and this prompted my subconscious to decide that if this were to be the case it would protect me by making me avoid trying in future.

Now I feel differently. I will risk losing because it makes me a better person if I can handle both the triumph of a win and the disaster of a loss and, in the words of Rudyard Kipling, "treat those two impostors just the same".

Summary

When we release the past we are able to discover the true potential within us.
Being in our brilliance means we do not crave the spotlight.
By being in our brilliance we allow others to shine.

MOSAIC Approach:	Examples:
Mission What do I want to achieve?	To let my brilliance shine.
Opportunity for improvement identified What areas in my life could do with improvement and change?	To let go of the need to be the centre of attention
Skills and abilities are assessed What am I able to do, what will require practice?	I can allow others to take the credit, but I may have to practice dumping the past so I can see who I really am beneath the nonsense.
Atmosphere is assessed What are things like around me? How supportive are family/friends/colleagues?	I am always the life and soul of the party, and yet feel vulnerable about my friends not liking me.
Impact of changes are considered Will there be problems, if so what are they likely to be and can I deal with them?	I may have to dare to lose to win in order to discover if my friends really do like me as I am.
Catalyst What can I do to speed changes into place? What will work as a catalyst for me?	The Phoenix Exercise should help me to discover who I am, and then I will keep affirming my brilliance to myself in my head until it becomes second nature.

"Change Thinking" Assignments   ✓

Affirm "I love my own company". Recognise when you are "shining".	
Use the Native American view, we belong to the earth, it does not belong to us.	
Remember you were a beloved baby once, full of all the potential that every infant carries. That precious baby is still within you.	
Waking Mantra:	
I am enough, and enough is a feast.	

"Take Action" Assignments   ✓

Give recognition to others, you do not have to own all the ideas.	
Peel back the layers of your heart and be prepared to have a good cry – have you suppressed this? Tears won't last forever and they will allow you to free yourself of the past.	
Find your brilliance, get into it and get out of the spotlight. Lead by allowing others to shine.	
Look at pictures of you as a baby and learn to love that little infant with all your heart.	
Dare to Lose to Win, take chances by letting go of the need to be a success. Visualise your success; and success will surely follow.	
Make a point of balancing your life, work, family, friends, etc	

Chapter 11
Step 5 - Angel of Truth

Discover:
How to antidote the Guilt Vampire.
How to feel authentic emotions and create fulfilling relationships.

How to antidote the Guilt Vampire:

By using the principles of simple truth I can lose the need for guilt and discover that I can gain energy from being congruent.

Antidote to the Guilt Vampire:
The Angel of Truth represents our ability to deal with life simply and honestly. When this angel is awakened within us we are able to be congruent, the same on the inside as we are on the outside.

On the surface the Guilt Vampire is a martyr, suffering for us all, prepared to put itself to the back of the queue so that we can benefit; it gets what it wants by making us feel guilty, often in very subtle and almost invisible ways. The Guilt Vampire has a kindly face, the face of a benevolent mother, and so it can be called the maternal Vampire. However, under this are the terrifying features of a raging vampire in the midst of its fury. The Guilt Vampire hides the face of anger.

How do we antidote the Guilt Vampire within?
Soup is a comforting and warming food, and garlic is cleansing and healthy. When we use garlic it clears the sinuses and allows us to breathe easily. It cleanses the blood and allows us to feel vital and well.

To rid ourselves of the inner Guilt Vampire we need to regularly take a metaphorical bowl of 'Garlic Soup'; this is the simplest recipe, there are no special secret ingredients, it is just garlic and water simmered for some time so that the authentic taste can be appreciated. Garlic soup may take a little getting used to; it is an acquired taste. In the same way working from simple truth takes a little getting used to, but in the end it is nourishing to our lives.

By drinking in the truth, recognising the needs we have and calmly stating them we are able to remove that constriction that we feel, we are able to breathe in life and live it to the fullest. We can make as much Garlic Soup as we like, and pour it upon everyone who comes into our lives. We may have to expect the odd cynic, just as Snow White's purity was resented by the wicked Witch Queen, but in the end it will win through against our own vampires as well as against the vampire in others.

When we bathe the wounds of our relationships in purifying soup we enable the relationship to grow and thrive. But when we do not, the relationship festers, and old hurts become niggles that in turn become nasty sores. We become bitter, and the relationship may either die completely or survive, but in an unhealthy and dissatisfactory state.

Fig 11.1 Use GARLIC to repel them:

First, to use garlic, you need to have an awareness of your own inner Guilt Vampires, then, if you notice your energy depleting, use the following acronym to remind you of the steps to take:

Guilt on hold - When you feel a sense of guilt, stop. Decide to put this on hold while you follow the next steps.

Activate awareness - Become aware of potential vampirism and make conscious decisions and choices. Do not be thrown into reactive behaviour. In other words, work from the things you can change, and not the things you cannot. You cannot change the vampire's behaviour, but you can change your own.

Resist Reacting - When we try to react in the right way we almost always get it wrong and create greater discomfort for ourselves. Or we practice appropriate reactions and they fail to work too. When we are faced with a vampiric communication exchange, resist any reaction at all. In other words, when they push your buttons, stop, take a breath, and *do not react at all*.

Language, use it carefully - It is not only what you say, but, most importantly, how you say it. You can easily find yourself using language that betrays emotional hurts or manipulation. Avoid blame, take responsibility for yourself. Use the "simple truth" approach and keep people enlightened. In this way you will not find them lurking in the shadows of half truths and rumours.

Instincts -Trust yourself, maintain your faith in yourself, be self approving. You do not need validation from the vampire.

Control your energy flow -Keep something back. Do not be overly ready to reveal your inner most hurts or to discover theirs. Do not let the Guilt Vampire across the threshold.

Use GARLIC to repel them:

Garlic, known to repel vampires, is also well known for its healing and health giving powers.

It represents the ability to provide simple love. In others words, in a business setting, this simple remedy can be applied by listening without judgement, supporting to enable empowerment without being manipulated, recognition of the value of the individual without trying to force him or her to fit into a category etc. The simple GARLIC mnemonic will help you to remember how to respond to vampirism.

How to feel authentic emotions and create fulfilling relationships.

Rather than trying to hide our feelings of guilt, fear and anger we can instead understand and experience our authentic feelings and discover how this will create a simple truth that will strengthen all our relationships.

Snow White and the Wicked Queen:

The Guilt Vampire can be seen in the story of Snow White. Here the Guilt Vampire has two faces, the beautiful and benevolent face of the Step Mother and Queen, and the ugly, gnarled and evil face of the witch or crone.

It is interesting that old age is often used to indicate evil, with witches portrayed as "ugly" because they have the traits of aging and have lost the beauty of their youth. Interestingly, many "modern witches" believe that to see the beauty within we have to see beyond the effects of aging. I remember once hearing a radio story about an old man who was sitting looking at his wife as she lay close to death. In that moment he recalled their happy life together and realised that her entire life had been leading up to this moment, when she was her ultimate self, her true and most beautiful self. This was her completion in his eyes.

The Wicked Queen is obsessed by her own "skin deep" beauty, and it is her fear that Snow White, in her purity, is more beautiful than she, that motivates her to try to destroy Snow White.

However, her ugliness is a function of the lie that she is living, and this will always seep through in the end, as we know that the wicked Queen can never win over the purity of Snow White. This does not stop the Queen from trying, however.

Snow White represents the simplicity and purity of the truth, and although the Queen may momentarily strike her down, her honesty ensures that she survives in the end.

The Queen is afraid of her own ugliness, and yet cannot find beauty within.

However lovely she is on the surface she will only be truly beautiful if she is the same on the inside.

Snow White's innocence makes her a perfect victim to the Queen, and yet it is also this perfect trust that saves her in the end. Snow White has to die to be reborn; in dying she has the ultimate moments of total peace from which she can awaken, refreshed and mature without the need to be cared for.

The Queen's inner ugliness causes her to transform into a monstrous beast, which is ultimately destroyed forever.

Fig 11.2 Case Study: Harry

Harry had telephoned his father to tell him about his success at work. He was delighted to have been able to take on a new employee, Jane, who would be able to reduce his workload and allow him to focus on the things in which he was interested.

Harry told his father that Jane would be supervising the team, to which his father replied, "That's nice for her, she can have a cup of coffee and watch the team working". Harry was really cross about the reaction, which was clearly meant to undermine Jane and which consequently undermined him and his judgement too. Harry did not want to have an argument with his father, so instead found himself justifying Jane and her work.

On ending the call, Harry felt annoyed that his father had created this reaction in him. He wondered why he had felt obliged to respond at all. Perhaps he should have allowed the comment to go unchecked. In other words, he could have "ignored the nonsense".

Blame:

The Queen blames Snow White because the Magic Mirror tells her that it is Snow White and not she who is "Fairest of them all".

In order to awaken our angel we need to take responsibility for our feelings, and communicate honestly, rather than searching for the blame in others.

When the Queen realises that Snow White is not dead as she had instructed, she becomes furious, her anger distorts her and changes her to an evil beast, the personification of her emotions.

Incongruence:

Congruence is harmony, it relates to things in balance. When we are being congruent all our messages match our feelings, we say what we mean, we say how we feel, we state what we want and need. The Guilt Vampire is afraid of saying what it feels or what it wants because it doesn't feel it deserves attention; it feels a need to demonstrate that it is a deserving case. A Vampire does this by claiming that it is unable to cope, it feels unwell or that it is out of its depth (although "carrying on regardless"). It makes it absolutely clear that whatever it must do will be extremely difficult, but that it will suffer (though not so much in silence).

The Dangerous side:

The Guilt Vampire is a heaving mass of dangerous emotions under an innocuous and lovely façade. We see it as kind and benevolent but in fact we are manipulated by its incongruent emotions.

Because the Guilt Vampire refuses to admit to its emotions they become stored up on the inside. It uses guilt to get its own way, and yet under the surface is full of anger, fear, sadness and, indeed, its own guilt.

When these emotions go unexpressed they poison the person and create bitterness. Vlad the Slayer, the mythical person upon whom the story of Dracula is based, apparently chose his cruel lifestyle as a result of a loss in love. The most pernicious Vampire may have originated from being unable to express emotions that it felt were a sign of its weakness. The Queen in Snow White is a perfect example of bitterness personified. She becomes a terrible creature, distorted and deformed by her jealousy and bitterness.

In fact, it takes courage to express feelings, and the idea that people are weaker for being emotional is a travesty and an untruth. Not only does expression of emotions increase your mental and physical health, it is also part of you as a whole person. Real weakness is seen in the vampire who cannot resist its dark longings, not in the person who is prepared to risk all to feel their feelings fully.

Authentic Emotions:

In order to free ourselves of the Guilt Vampire we need to understand that we have emotions and be able to feel them. Rather than trying to put a lid on feelings, the Angel of Truth recognises and accepts that it has feelings. It feels them to the core of its being. This can be quite scary, because it may feel that it will lose itself in the emotion. But this is not true; feeling an emotion does not mean that we become the emotion.

The Angel flies above the feeling; it feels it and then moves on, it is not tied to the ground by feelings. However the Vampire is shackled to an emotion it cannot reveal; this is like a millstone around its neck. It cannot take off and fly because it is weighed down, and the more weighed down by hidden emotions it feels, the greater the weight.

Acknowledging feelings:

Acknowledging our feelings does not mean we have to demonstrate them. We can tell our partner that we feel angry without being angry. We can say that we feel sad without crying. It is not necessary to demonstrate the emotion but we can still acknowledge it. Once we have acknowledged how we feel we can then state how we feel to others.

Non Authentic Emotions:
Strategies we use to maintain the Guilt Vampire will include denial, failing to express ourselves, and feeling overcome by emotions.

When we deny how we really feel we have to invent greater and greater "lies" to explain to ourselves what is going on inside. These usually involve finding ways of pinning the blame on our partner. Denial makes us unhappy and stressed, it is a fulltime occupation to maintain the inner lie; we cannot let our guard down for a moment.

Failing to express ourselves is the result of feeling we are not of value and that our feelings are therefore not of value. This business of subjugating the self is unhealthy and, moreover, a contradiction to our beliefs.

As Guilt Vampires we would say that we were of less importance than others, we seek to serve others, and see ourselves as less deserving. However, if we see humans as deserving, it makes no sense to say, "all humans are deserving and valuable, except for me, I am less deserving and less valuable than any others". And yet, that is precisely what the Inner Guilt Vampire says. It makes us feel guilty, and so we use other strategies, because in the end, we crave love and cannot be fulfilled by the shallow existence we have as lower forms of life. This results in a swing between being obsequious and lowly, putting ourselves down and giving more than we receive, to feeling angry and aggrieved when people take advantage of us.

One of the most shocking aspects of Aldous Huxley's book "A Brave New World" is the revelation that society creates low forms of life, hideously deformed to suit a horrific working existence in mines. To maintain the status quo the people are given the drug "Soma" which keeps them in blissful ignorance, and is highly addictive.

We are shocked by the idea that some human beings can subjugate others in so shocking and cruel a way, and yet we do this to ourselves all the time. We feed ourselves upon the Soma of other people's guilt, allowing them to feed us with energy to alleviate the misery of being what we may perceive ourselves to be, an insignificant and pointless human being.

Apologies that make you feel worse:
When our vampire is at full swing it is extremely clever at turning a "lose" situation into a "vampiric win". In other words, the Guilt Vampire will say sorry, but in such a way that the apology seems to make us feel worse than before. The Guilt Vampire actually likes "losing" because it can turn this into a vampire win. The Guilt vampire will enjoy being, in its opinion, less clever than you, or less attractive, or less skilful or less likeable than you.

When a vampire apologises it is being manipulative, the apology is for no other purpose than to be "passively aggressive", that is, by proving its inferiority, the vampire wins because it has power over you by commanding the feelings, and invoking the guilt. It is aggressive as it rides roughshod over your rights, but it is passive, because it is covert, hidden and feels almost impossible to handle.

Mortgaging the soul:

When we are in the clutches of the Guilt Vampire we may feel as though we have mortgaged our soul. As with a conventional mortgage, this one feels as though it is offering us security, it feels as though we are being given a gift. However, also like the conventional mortgage we give back at least twice what we are provided with, and it can be withdrawn at any time. This feeling that the mortgage can be "called in" makes us more vulnerable than we realise, because on a day-to-day basis we do not even imagine that this could happen. However, one small mistake, one occasion when we do not make our regular payment into the vampire's account, and the vampire will make unreasonable demands. The Vampire Mortgagor will demand its pound of flesh; make you feel guilty if you do not give in.

It is very likely to draw your attention to the small print of your relationship. When you assess this small print it would probably imply the need for you to behave in ways that would support your vampire friend or relative; with little support the other way round. However, the Vampire Mortgagor will very cleverly tell you why your helping it is actually a benefit to you!

State your needs:

We all have needs, and when we are behaving congruently we are happy to state those needs. When we can do this we free ourselves of the Vampire and find that we are able to enhance our relationships by bringing them into truth.

Angelic Voices Case Study:

I had a consistently bad back, and it would ache most in the evenings. When I was sitting resting and would feel like having a cup of tea I would ask my partner if he would like one himself. If he said yes, I would struggle to my feet and go and get one for him and myself. Of course, by the time I had got up he was offering to help me, "Its OK, I will get it for you", "Oh, no, no, I'm alright" I would protest. And I would keep protesting until eventually he would settle me back onto my chair and get me my tea and anything else I needed or wanted.

Sometimes, however, he would ignore me and my overacting, and then I would feel overcome with resentment (in silence). I would make even more fuss of my poor aching back.

The strange thing is, my back really did hurt, and was quite debilitating.

Eventually I realised that I was consistently allowing my vampire to rise from the grave and so I decided to awaken my angel instead. The angel would state the truth, simply and without manipulation; "Would you mind getting me a cup of tea, I would really appreciate it, as my back is aching".

Amazingly to me, rather than resenting me for asking, my partner was delighted to be able to do something caring for me. He was glad to help, and felt he was making a choice and not being manipulated into it.

Now, something even more wonderful has happened. I no longer get bad backache. It is as though my subconscious no longer requires this behaviour, as I am now able to state my needs without relying on my "poor health" as an excuse or reason.

Giving Feedback:

If we are to employ angelic behaviours we need to remember that in giving feedback we must concentrate on what the person does and not upon what we believe or imagine they are; in other words, the behaviours our partner demonstrates, not our partner him/herself. This means using adverbs, which relate to actions, (what was done) and not adjectives which relate to qualities, (what he or she is like).

When we need to give feedback to people we must be sure we use the mnemonic FEEDBAC. This simple-to-remember approach will help to ensure that you do not cause either your vampire or your partner's to appear. Feedback should be:

> Focused upon what can be used
> Experienced and observed by us, and not hearsay
> Essentials—the specifics
> Description of the behaviour and not judgement
> Behaviours that *we have seen* demonstrated
> Alterable things
> Contributing information and sharing ideas

Visualisation:

The single most effective method for changing behaviours is through *visualisation*. The art of visualisation is simply the use of the imagination, but this goes beyond simply seeing the images in your head. You need to see, hear and feel the experience.

The FEEDBAC Model in the workplace for giving Angelic Feedback Fig. 11.3		
Focused	**Vampiric Behaviour**	**Angelic Behaviour**
Only give the amount of information the receiver can use; even if this is substantially less than we would like to give.	And another thing...."	"There are a few areas we should talk about, but let's concentrate on this one......"
Experienced and Observed		
What is it that we actually *observed* being done. Do not be tempted to make inferences such as why they did it. Do not rely on hearsay.	"I know you are trying to make an effort to please that customer but according to the others you did not really secure the sale in the first place."	"I noticed you gave this customer a higher than usual discount."
Essentials		
Again, concentrating on the specifics of the behaviour, and not generalising.	"The whole place is a mess, and you have to sort it out immediately as I must be ready for my sales presentation."	"The desks need to be cleared, and the top shelf needs tidying. I need to have it organised for my presentation on Friday."
Description not Judgement		
Clearly and concisely describe what was done without making a judgement.	"I want to talk to you about your slapdash approach to cooking the sauce."	"I would like to talk to you about the way in which you have cooked the bechamel sauce."
Behaviours we have seen		
Negative feedback must not attack the person, but should only refer to what he/she has done.	You're stupid to put the files in your drawer. What are you? Yes, stupid. How would you expect me to find them? Eh?	I found the files in your top right hand drawer; they should be replaced in the filing cabinet each time they are removed.
Alterable Behaviour		
Only give information about behaviour the receiver is able to change.	"I don't like the way you speak, can't you try to act and sound a bit more *intelligent*?"(!)	"When you speak to Mr Jones try to remember to use this check-list, and speak as clearly as possible."
Contribute Ideas/Information		
Try to avoid judgmental expressions like 'don't' 'never' 'always' when giving feedback. Instead use expressions that are personal, "I felt...." "I thought...."	"You look and sound wrong in front of the customer, it will never help you to make sales."	I feel it may help if you didn't look so intense, I think it is better to stand a little further back, for example, and I find I have to ensure that I am not frowning or looking too stern.."

Practise visualising situations *before they happen* creating a positive outcome. In your visualisation you should see yourself behaving angelically and achieving the outcome you desire.

It is quite normal for your subconscious self doubts to reveal themselves through difficulties and problems in your visualisation. For example, you may find the person with whom you are communicating in your visualisation becomes argumentative. If your mind throws up these kinds of barriers, use visualisation to overcome them one by one, but keep going until you succeed. Remember, this is just your inner vampire trying to distract you!

Positive Affirmations:

Ideally, start each day by developing a positive state of mind. So begin by looking at yourself in the mirror and telling yourself how positive you feel, that is, begin with a positive affirmation. The following is an example of a *'Positive Affirmation'*:

"Today and everyday, I am positive and am able to awaken the angel within me, I achieve my desired outcomes, I am relaxed and effective".

You should do these 'Positive Affirmations' regularly and often. Try saying them ten times each day. They are called positive affirmations because they concentrate on positive aspects; "I am" as opposed to, "I am not". They embed the statement in your subconscious as though it were fact. As a result, your behaviours alter imperceptibly and the affirmation becomes true.

It is not necessary for you to believe it is true, it is only necessary for you to make the statement, and do so emphatically. The rest follows naturally.

Whenever you are under pressure in the day, quickly draw upon your affirmation. Take a deep breath and let it out slowly, and as you do so repeat the affirmation in your head. When you have finished it add:

"My angel is awakened and I am now ready to face any situation."

Process of Awakening the Angel of Truth Fig 11.4		
Vampire	Responsibility	Angel
I can't	I won't	I will

Case Study: Declining overtime

This case study demonstrates how Jill used visualisation to alter her outcomes.

My boss wanted me to do some overtime, but I did not want to do it. I decided that before confronting her I needed to visualise a good outcome for us both.

Visualisation—Before the event: During my visualisation I stated firmly to my boss that I did not want to do overtime on this occasion, and she happily accepted my view and said she would ask someone else.

Results – After the event: I felt confident about saying no and my boss said that she had already found someone else, and thanked me for being upfront. She said she would ask me again as she knew I would give an honest answer regarding whether I could or wanted to do it. She said she that she felt we had an excellent working relationship, and then, believe it or not, thanked me! I was thrilled and now feel really good about my work and my job.

Why refuse to accept a compliment graciously?

As victims we have a poor self image, believing we are unworthy of kindness and that we can never compete with others. However, as mature adults we can face the world without playing games to gain attention.

Refusing a compliment is an example of vampirism, and, although it virtually never works, we tend to use the same tactic again and again. Without consciously meaning to, many people refuse a compliment because they have low self esteem, and do not believe that anyone could really mean it, they want further reassurance: "No, it *really* does look nice, honestly". To help you, think of compliments like gifts. Imagine responding to a compliment in exactly the same way as you would if someone gave a gift or offered a chocolate to you.

If you say, "I'm on a diet, I would refuse a chocolate anyway", note that this is a smoke screen. Compliments are only notional chocolates; it is the principle of the issue, not the practise. So make that Vampire get back into the coffin.

If you say, "I would refuse a gift" it is again the vampire rising. How would you feel if someone refused your gift? Hurt? Disappointed? Try to understand how important it is to accept graciously, as it makes the giver feel good too. Compliments are gifts, accept them as such. When someone thanks you say "You're welcome", rather than "Don't thank me, it was nothing".

Why can't we say "No"?

Why do we find it so difficult to say "no" or to make a request? The folllowing examples demonstrate some of the expectations we may have and how we can change our perception of them.

Fig 11.5 What does your response mean? Do you reply to a compliment in any of the following ways? If so, consider the hidden message:

What you say to a compliment	What it implies about the compliment
"What, this old thing?" "It wasn't that difficult to do"	"I don't deserve it."
"You don't really think I look nice, do you?" "My work really isn't *that* good"	"You don't really mean it."
"You look very nice today as well" "I think the work *you* did was far better"	"I can't receive without giving you a present in return."
"I'm sure you say that to everyone!"	"You give gifts to everyone, don't you? So I'm not important at all."

Altering Perceptions:
"If I refuse they will be terribly disappointed."
Take responsibility for *your* problem and not *theirs*. If your refusal is delivered with concern for the feelings of the other person, but with calm and congruent (honest) communication they are less likely to take it badly or be deeply affected. Be the same on the inside as you are on the outside.
We all have disappointments at some time in our life and, as we know, weakness can be used to manipulate. You are not helping these vampires if you allow them to take control of you by playing at being hurt. But then again, is it their vampire or is it your own that has risen?
"They may not like me any more."
At work, well, they may not for a while. If it does last, does it matter? Why?
Realistically, this is an excuse not a reason. A real friend will not be so fickle as to end a relationship on one refusal. If they do, then it shows them to be a poor friend; good job you found out now! The same applies to work. Your superior is sure to want you to feel positive about any work you are asked to undertake.
"It must be important or they would not have asked."
How do you know it is as important as you assume? Are their needs more important than your own? They may prefer to know how you really feel.
They may find it easier to ask someone a favour if they know they will only do it if they are happy to, and not grudgingly. After all, they probably want to retain your friendship / good will as much as you want to retain theirs.
Your boss will not want you to do a job badly because you feel angry about having to do it. Maybe there are other possibilities, sharing the task etc. How will you know if you avoid facing the issue?

Moving from Vampire to Angel:

The typical stance of the Guilt Vampire is "Can't". In other words, "*I can't* say "No"." "*I can't* ask them." "*I can't* change." Using the word "can't" is another way to avoid taking responsibility. When we say, "I can't" we mean it is not in our power to do or say this thing.

To awaken our Angel of Truth we need to accept that it *is* in our power, that we have the choice. If we can make a small step from avoiding responsibility to accepting responsibility we will realise that it is not a matter of "can't" but of "won't". From this position we accept that we *have the power*, but choose not to use it. *"I can say 'no', but I won't."*. The next step is to use the techniques we learn to open up our choices further. Now you have two responses: to say yes, or no, instead of only one. *"I can say "no", and sometimes I will"*.

Love:

Steven Covey (Seven Habits of Highly Effective People) describes Love as a verb as well as an adjective. When we employ love as a verb we become satisfied and energised by it; in other words, when love becomes something we *do* and not just something we feel.

Many relationships end up on the skids because a partner complains he or she does not feel loved any more and therefore does not feel s/he loves his or her partner. And yet, if we begin to change our attitude towards love, thinking of it as something we do, rather than something we expect to feel, we can create positive changes that liberate us from feeling love is passing us by. It will enable us to feel energised, vibrant and "in love" with our relationship again.

Exercise in Love as a Verb (1):

When was the last time you complained about someone you love, or used to love? Consider the nature of the complaint. Did you complain about something they did or did not do? How did this make you feel? What was your response to the situation? Did you:

- Complain about what he or she did, and how you felt about it?
- Attempt to improve your partner by giving instructions on "a better way"?
- Become upset?
- Remember to do something kind and loving for your partner?

The first three are typical responses and demonstrate the idea that we consider love to be a feeling we have. When we don't get that feeling we seek to blame the other party and instruct them, complain to them or use emotional tactics such as being upset to demonstrate to them how we *feel*.

Exercise in Love as a Verb (2):

Consider the above exercise and write down a list of things that you expect the person or people you love to do. Note everything you expect from them. The following examples may help you:

I expect the people I love to .... never lose their temper.

I expect the people I love to .... appreciate everything I do.

I expect the people I love to .... listen to my advice and be thankful for it.

Now release them from your narrow range of expectations and note ways in which you can demonstrate love to people through what you do and say.

For example: *I can* release people from my expectations and can *demonstrate love to them by...being patient, listening, not reacting, showing love etc*

Being Totally Present:

Being with people you love is an energising experience. Sometimes the people we love drain us through vampirism, so companionship should always be sought with people with whom you have a mutual energy exchange.

When energy flows between people it creates a synergy, in other words, this flow creates an additional energy of its own which is beneficial to both; both gain and neither lose. The biggest problem is in recognising when synergy is taking place, rather than a sapping of one party's energy.

Synergy can only happen when both partners are "totally present in the moment". In other words, they both have full attention on what is happening at that moment, neither "wander" to write imaginary shopping lists, or to become sidetracked by irrelevances.

Being totally present is not the same as active listening. Active Listening is a technique; it involves making eye contact, nodding and "uh huh-ing" at the speaker. I am personally not fond of Active Listening as it implies that we only have to use "techniques" to improve communication. We can use Active Listening methods and still be only half present; we can remain thinking about our next question, or drifting off, mentally.

Altering communication from judgement and blame to ownership and responsibility. Fig. 11.6		
Judgement and Blame		
Disowning: You	**Emotion:** make me feel (angry)	**Description of behaviour:** when you do that.
Owning and Communicating		
Owning: I	**Emotion:** feel (angry)	**Description of behaviour:** when you do that

Real listening involves letting go of all the nonsense that fills our heads and just being with the person who is speaking. That means we exist only in that moment, with no future or past, and only with that person. When we do this, then we are being "totally present".

Exercise: Recognising an Energy Synergy

Try this: Sit opposite another person, so close that you are touching. Look straight into your partner's eyes. Then speak for five minutes without either of you losing eye contact, even for a moment. You should speak about yourself, but under no circumstances must you say anything negative; everything must be positive. You can talk about your achievements, family, hobbies, personality, preferences; whatever you speak about the rule remains—it must be positive.
When you have completed the exercise swap roles.
Then consider: How did it feel to be listening? How did it feel to be speaking? What happened to your energy? Many people will experience an energy synergy. In other words, both experiences create additional energy in the partners. This will only happen if you are *totally present with your partner.*
If you do not have a partner to work with, try this experiment in front of the mirror. Although you may not achieve the same feelings, you may discover that you can be self energising and that you can help yourself to feel loved.

Exercise: Creating Energy Synergy Opportunities

Consider a situation when you were angry with another person. Write it down. Then look at the example in fig 11.6 and see if your communication demonstrated owning the emotion or disowning and blaming.
Now re-write the experience and alter the words. Try experimenting by practising this in front of the mirror. What do you notice? How do you think your partner would have responded? Now put this method of communicating and thinking into practice.

Keeping feelings in:

We tend to hold our emotions like shells within us, with our most preferred emotion on "top" and the others in successive layers under the surface. The uppermost emotion is the one we reveal most readily; perhaps this was the one that was most rewarded or praised when we were children.
The key emotions are Happiness, Anger, Sadness and Fear. Perhaps it is also worth considering jealousy and greed. Which do you put on the outside? Which is hidden so far inside that you hardly would know that it was there at all?

Feeling our Feelings:

Feeling joyful does not require you to deny your feelings. Quite the reverse, you can accept how you are feeling, and then move on. When we can accept and feel our emotions we can then say "I feel sad right now, and I am living in this moment and it is wonderful to be alive". We know that the feeling is going to pass, and that it is adding to our wholeness as a person.

We are able to stop manipulating others when we feel the true and authentic feelings that we have within us, and by doing so we allow them to become free, we no longer tie them to our soul and allow them to pull us down deeper and deeper into the dread world of the House of Horrors.

Sometimes we believe we do feel our feelings, but we are trapped in only one way of feeling. For every feeling we use the same emotion. For example, some people become angry when they have been hurt. Sadness or vulnerability may be more appropriate, but instead they choose an emotion in which they feel they have competence, perhaps anger.

Likewise, some people will burst into tears and feel sad when they are afraid, or when they are angry. There are even those, who when faced with happiness will find a reason to be sad about it.

In order to awaken the angel of truth we need to feel all our feelings, and this means we must be brave, because it is much easier to avoid feeling altogether.

Case Study: Clara

Clara delightedly announced to her family that she was pregnant. Her mother's reaction was to burst into tears and claim that "her little girl" was lost to her forever! Fortunately, Clara was aware of her mother's responses and "ignored the nonsense". In fact her mother, being extremely maternal by nature, was thrilled about the prospect of having a grandchild, but she had not yet learnt how to feel her feelings.

Feeling alive:

What gives meaning to your life? Whatever your answer may be, it will probably be linked to a feeling. If your loved ones give meaning, perhaps it is because of the feelings that are evoked in you when you think about them or spend time with them. If it is your work, perhaps it is the thrill of the challenge and the feeling of satisfaction.

We all have feelings and they drive us. It is time to accept this fact of life and enjoy it. Holding onto or trying to control feelings so that we fit a narrow view of what is right, or acceptable or even professional will only cause our own development to be stunted. We grow only in one direction, and end up emotionally deformed, just like the Witch in Snow White.

When we fully experience all our feelings, we may have to accept that some will not feel that pleasant, but when we are feeling at least we know that we are alive. When we stop feeling altogether we have become the undead, and we are walking with the vampires.

What are the benefits of authentic feelings?

When we do not feel authentic feelings we do not know how to value what we have in our lives. For example, many people remain in miserable relationships because they believe they feel love for the partner who is abusing them. When we are able to get in touch with real emotions we can find that our feelings of love are actually a mixed mess of many other sensations, these may be pride, wishful thinking, loyalty, fear and addiction. "Feeling real feelings" may mean we have to grieve over the loss of some of our relationships.

Angelic Voices Case Study: Jackie Fig 11.7

When Jackie lost her husband her first response was to throw herself into her work. She did not take any time for her grief. Without realising it, Jackie had become bad tempered and nit picking, constantly finding fault in others and demoralising everyone in the office. However, after finding that things were going very badly in her job, and after much encouragement from her boss, she decided to go for counselling. She was not at all keen, and after three sessions she found herself dreading going to the weekly meetings. She explained to her counsellor that she was afraid of the meetings because she knew she would have "to feel". The problem with feeling was that she could only imagine feeling sad, she was afraid that she would lose herself in grief. Her counsellor urged her to "get into her grief" even if this was uncomfortable.

Jackie sat at home one night with a cup of tea and thought about her husband . She allowed herself to admit how much she missed him and began to cry. She had to do this a couple of times before she was really able to throw herself into the grief. She wept for two hours with only a few brief breaks, which seemed to occur about every fifteen minutes or so.

Then she stopped. She was not able to feel intensely emotional any more. She dried her eyes and made another cup of tea. She drank this quietly and then went to bed and slept and slept. Jackie awoke so late she was not able to get into work on time, and did not arrive until nearly lunchtime. She explained to her boss, and luckily, he was sympathetic and pleased that she had made real progress. Jackie continued to have moments of intense grief, but realised these lasted only fifteen to twenty minutes each time. She did not lose herself, but she did feel energised and alive, and, was eventually able to go on to make new relationships.

Remaining in control:

Can we lose control if we begin to feel all our feelings? Many people fear that they will lose themselves in grief, that they will never be able to rise above the sadness of a lost love, whether the love has been lost through death or through the end of a relationship. Some even feel the same about a lost job.

When a relationship ends and we do not allow ourselves to go through the process of grief we will perpetually be under the spell of our ex-lover or former employer etc.

We need to go through the grief process, sometimes many more times than just once. For many the process will be similar to Fig 11.7 and it can circle in either direction or leap stages or even invent some new ones!

Grief needs to be felt in order to allow us to move on. If we run back to the cause of the pain, we only give ourselves more in the end. Often it is monumentally hard to give up a relationship, even when it does not serve us at all. However, we will not lose ourselves in grief. You can feel emotions and still be capable of rational thought and action. For example, even if you are furious you are still able to make a decision if you need to, even if you are beside yourself with grief, you could still deal with a child with a cut knee.

Exercise: Feeling authentic emotions

Make a list of all the different possible emotions. Have you managed to get at least 100 different ones? If not, keep adding to the list whenever you can. Review your list of emotions. How good are you at feeling each of these? Are you very good at feeling anger, but not too good at feeling sad? Or vice versa perhaps? At any possible moment in the day ask yourself "how am I feeling now?" and notice it. In this way you will soon become aware of your real emotions and begin to experience authentic feelings as they arise.

Feeling Intense Emotions:

We are unable to sustain intense emotions for longer than fifteen to twenty minutes on the whole. Even if we have a break and then resume the feeling, we cannot maintain that intensity for much longer than twenty minutes. Knowing this helps us to accept that we will not lose our self in an emotion, and that we can still be in control even when we feel intensively.

Fearing losing control:

We do not have to fear losing control of ourselves. Practice feeling intensely with the knowledge that you can retain control. If you say "I get out of control" you are creating that pattern for yourself before you start. Whereas, if you say to yourself "I can be intensely emotional and remain aware of myself and in control of my actions" you will realise that this is possible.

When you have moments of extreme emotion, you will realise that feeling does not prevent you from thinking, and that the thinking part of you still works. As previously mentioned, we need to stop the thinking *from preventing the feeling* (cutting off the vampire's head!) but interestingly this does not stop the intellectual part from working. In fact, it is able to work far better, because it works with the whole person, and not a few jumbled thoughts that are out of context with the emotions.

Summary

The simple truth will cure our relationships of manipulation through guilt. This means being congruent, that is, the same on the inside as the outside.

By experiencing the full range of our feelings we are able to bring self-knowledge and honesty with ourselves into our lives.

When we are able to be honest with ourselves we can be honest with others and allow our relationships thrive.

Feeling authentic emotions frees us from the danger of bitterness, which comes from unexpressed anger, sadness and fear.

We can be honest with people without upsetting them by using the FEEDBAC model.

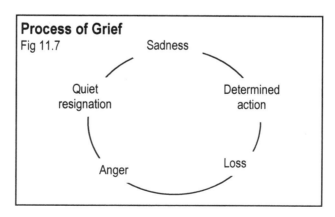

Process of Grief
Fig 11.7 — Sadness, Determined action, Loss, Anger, Quiet resignation

MOSAIC Approach:	Examples:
Mission What do I want to achieve?	Feel my feelings without being out of control.
Opportunity for improvement identified What areas in my life could do with improvement and change?	I have difficulty dealing with my mother, and always rise to the bait at the least provocation.
Skills and abilities are assessed What am I able to do, what will require practise?	I know I am good at feeling anger but very poor at feeling sadness– I avoid it at all costs.
Atmosphere is assessed What are things like around me? How supportive are family/friends/colleagues?	My mother loves me unconditionally, so I should be able to work with her on this one. I have siblings that can support me too.
Impact of changes are considered Will there be problems, if so what are they likely to be and can I deal with them?	My mother may take offence, and I may end up getting mad with her. I need to prepare myself and not be put off by any strange tactics she may employ.
Catalyst What can I do to speed changes into place? What will work as a catalyst for me?	Spend more time with my mother, this should help to speed changes as we will get used to each other and our new ways of being, and feel more secure together.

"Change Thinking" Assignments

Be prepared to accept a compliment unconditionally.	
Notice every time you "suffer" and ask yourself, "Has this been a useful strategy in getting what I want? Squash martyrdom now.	
Waking Mantra:	
"I am secure in knowing that my needs will be answered."	

"Take Action" Assignments– Tips

You do not need to react to everything. Avoid responding to manipulation.	
Note what you feel when you feel it; get used to feeling authentic emotions.	
Notice when you blame and develop your ability to respond (responsibility)	
Use the FEEDBAC model to be honest with people without upsetting them .	
Clearly ask for what you want.	

Chapter 12

Step 6—Angel of Love

Discover:
How to antidote the Advisor Vampire
How to awaken love

How to antidote the Advisor Vampire

I am in balance and unity, I give to others without trying to be an advisor. I create a synergy when I freely exchange energy with others.

Antidote to the Paternal Vampire: Balance and unity:
The Advisor Vampire may be our mentor and we may seek its advice, and it loves to give advice to us. It will thrill us with its fascinating ability to provide us with new insights on life; we become caught up on the fascinating way it speaks. The trouble with this mentor is that it finds the process of giving advice so thrilling that it captivates itself, but does not take its own advice!

The antidote to this vampire is balance and unity. We need to see ourselves as unified with and not separate from others, we are not better than they and we are not blessed with the answers to their woes. The antidote here is best described as "Physician, heal thyself", in other words, stop trying to fix everyone else, and sort out yourself. Our inner vampire will demonstrate to us that it is right; when our Advisor Vampire is at large we believe we are the only ones with the right answer, and can be furious with people who simply will not listen to us! We are often using methods that are completely devoid of balance, and so our Vampire will make judgements, comparisons and apportion blame.

How do we antidote the Advisor Vampire within?
This Vampire must receive a stake through the heart, because it believes it is separate, and it must be unified. We can only bring the two parts of its nature together by opening the heart and seeing the different parts for what they are, then we can grow back into human beings, with one unified heart.

A stake through the heart will expose the heart to the healing qualities of air, it will enable us to be open hearted, and will help us to unify our own heart with the hearts of all other human beings.

A Stake through the Heart:

In order to deactivate our vampire, only we can make the decision to stake our vampire through the heart. The heart represents both the seat of love and the seat of courage, as the word for courage is derived from the French for heart "coeur". Coeur sounds like "core", and perhaps this demonstrates how the heart is the centre or core of our life force.

"Big hearted" may describe someone who is generous and loving, and yet it can also mean brave and committed.

It is the heart that plays a big part in our ability to banish the vampire. The process of staking the heart is akin to opening it up so that we can expose our inner most self. Staking the heart with a wooden stake is relevant. Wood is non conductive, whereas a sword, being metal, could conduct. Therefore the sword is not inert, using the sword we could be transmitting energy to or from the slayer, allowing the energy to be rapidly drained away. In other words, the sword, which metaphorically represents air and thought, will not allow us to slay the vampire. The stake is blunt and natural. It connects us to the earth. The stake, which represents emotion and nature, will slay the vampire.

To use the stake means we have to open our hearts to love and be prepared to suffer a blow in the process. Even so, we cannot close our heart off, because to do so is to injure and not to heal.

If we close our hearts we prevent others from becoming close to us, we injure ourselves by being an island, unreachable and unlovable.

When the vampire's heart is staked, it allows the vampiristic part to die, and in the fiction, the face of the monster transforms back once more to the human face. The vampire becomes pure and peaceful again.

Being reborn:

This process of being "reborn" is vital to dealing with the vampires in our lives. We have to appreciate that staking our hearts carries with it pain, the pain of change, but remember also, that as we stake the unfeeling heart of the vampire, the pain we feel is the healing pain, as we reawaken our heart.

We are able to accept that when we feel pain it is OK because it is a part of the natural flow of life, to feel is to be alive. To be a vampire is to be unfeeling, unnatural and undead.

Holding onto emotion, failing to feel, failing to understand love without power, these are the elements of the vampire. To be human we need to feel joy and pain, be open to love in all events, even when it requires courage to do so.

Angelic Voices: Actor Martin Sheen

Martin Sheen, the film actor, who came to fame in the film Badlands and Apocalypse Now!, has spoken about his heart attack and how it changed his life. He saw his life as a cluster of fragments, without continuity or unity. When he suffered from a heart attack whilst filming "Apocalypse Now!" he felt he had an opportunity to "see the light" and pull the different aspects of his life together.

From this point he rebuilt his marriage, stopped drinking and became heavily involved in helping those less fortunate than himself, working with the Hispanic community and fighting for the rights of the downtrodden.

Martin Sheen's story is a perfect example of staking our vampire through the heart, and in his case, this is an almost literal interpretation of the metaphor. As he felt his own heart "shattering" so the fragments of his life could be seen for what they were. He felt at this point he had a choice, either to die or to live. The choice to live was not simply a choice to continue breathing, but a choice to understand what life really was; a gift that can be celebrated and lived to find joy and understanding in the world. For Martin Sheen this meant getting closer to God.

Life in Unity—Healthy Energy:

What is to live in unity? It is to be open to criticism without feeling disempowered by it, to be able to give love to one's partner without feeling the need to assert power over him or her. It is to share love with the community. Most importantly it is to understand that all of these things are part of ones wholeness, that they cannot be separated into fragments and still lived satisfactorily. They must be part of a unity within us and a vision of unity within the world.

Our health is determined by our attitude to ourselves. Heart attacks are a case in point. To save ourselves and our working community from disease we must pull the two parts of ourselves, of our heart, together. We must pull the two parts of our community together. The feeling heart and the working heart.

The working heart beats to pump the blood and keep us alive. Our feeling heart holds our emotions and has its own sense of itself. If the feeling heart is wounded, the working heart is stressed. This is true for individuals, but equally true for communities, businesses and families. If it is to create a rhythmic flow, the heart must be seen as one; strong, maintained and cared for.

Then, and only then can we have one heart, beating to the rhythm of our shared passions, the seat of love and courage. When we stake the heart, we need to recognise that the process of opening our heart in two should reveal both the tenderness of our feelings and the physical reality of our body in keeping us alive. The stress we create when we vampirise others can take its toll on both the feeling and the working heart. Martin Sheen's case study is the perfect example of this.

How to awaken love

When we are able to work from unity we can awaken love in ourselves and in others.

Awakening the Angel of Love:

How can we avoid becoming a vampire or a victim when we are trying to help others? For managers and those who advise and instruct others, including those "informal counsellors" who provide emotional support and guidance, the rule of thumb is to be sure you always hold back a little.

In other words, just because you feel you can advise it doesn't mean you should; holding back does not relate to love, but to the need to "tell". We must remain open to relationships, even if this seems dangerous, but being open doesn't mean drawing power from your position as adviser.

An understanding and awareness of Energy Vampires can demonstrably elevate communication in business and life to a whole new level. Where relations in the office support rather than feed off each other, office politics become void and businesses are able to grow new life through passion. Organisations that want to really progress today need to look into the possibility of vampires as destructive, but curable, forces within.

Wearing a Halo:

When you do communicate try filtering your words and deeds through your angelic halo. The Angel of Love becomes apparent in the words we speak and the way in which we live our lives. When we attach ourselves to the Sunshine of Joy we automatically find the Angel of Love rising up in us. It wants to make connections and we find ourselves drawn to others within whom this presence is growing, or already strong. We can recognise the Angel of Love at work within others and ourselves.

When we filter through the halo we become aware of the way in which our language betrays the gaps in our thinking. The three key gaps are based upon:

- Our Life Rules—the way *we* think life should be
- Generalisations—grand statements about what is true
- Comparators—Comparing one thing with another

Life Rules:

These are the rules by which we live our lives. We often create our Life Rules from within the House of Horrors; they may even be unwittingly imposed upon us. These rules demonstrate the way we think the world should be and begin with expressions like "People should always...", "You must never...", "Everybody is...", "Nobody should..." etc.

The words we use betray and, most importantly, reinforce our Life Rules. By using the word we strengthen the belief, or we create the belief from becoming involved with other people's Life Rules.

Change the way you communicate to change the way your think:			
Unfiltered Words	**Shining the Halo on the behaviour:**	**Filter**	**Adapted response**
Should	Life Rules — This can be demanding	Am I applying my rules to everyone else? Are my rules supporting me? Or are they impossible to live up to?	I should? What would happen if I didn't ...? Perhaps it is not necessary to ...
Everybody	Generalisations— This can be unrepresentative as it does not take into account individuality .	Am I generalising about life? Is this true or real?	Everybody? Some people
They			They? Who are they?
All			All? Well, some...
Always			Always? Often, or sometimes...
Never			Never? Usually not...
Better/ worse	Comparators— False comparisons are not like against like	Am I making true comparisons?	Better than what? Worse than what?
Hate Criticism	Damning/ Persecuting— Dictatorial attitude	Connect with authentic emotions	Instead of starting with "You are.." start with "I feel"
Its Terrible/Awful/ Appalling	Catastrophizing— Exaggeration	Describe behaviour rather than judge it:	"This is what has happened."
Aversion towards some people.	Prejudice- Having preconceptions	What is the real reason that I am reacting to this person?	"All people are of value—I see only the value in you."

Eric Berne described conversations in which we use these rules most extensively as "games" or "pastimes". In these games judgements are offered by all the participants, the conversation is carried out as though the truth is being spoken; for example it may be a group of women launching a tirade on "men" or vice versa. It could be a "discussion" about "the youth of today", or "single parent families" etc. People often joke that they have been "putting the world to rights", but often, and more worryingly, the participants may believe that their point of view *is* the right one.

Sometimes an individual can be the subject of this kind of "game", the group metaphorically circle someone, perhaps with criticisms or judgements about the way that individual should behave or look.

It is apparent when these games get underway as the individuals join in with rules and generalisations about groups of people, or even individuals.

The Angel of Love knows no rules:

The Angel of Love does not use Life Rules because it just is. It is not good and it is not bad, so it cannot determine what is right or wrong. At the same time, it does not have a head with a brain in it, so it does not go around thinking it is cleverer than everybody else.

When we awaken this presence within us, it spills out, we no longer need to attach labels that say "right" or "wrong" we just accept. This is how it is.

Generalisations:

When we decide that something that may be true for one must be true for all we are generalising. Do you like it when the generalisation is about yourself? Many of us do not because, we do not like to be placed in pigeonholes, but do we do this to others?

The Angel of Love does not generalise:

The Angel of Love does not generalise because it does not store useless information about who said what, and when. It does not troll out thoughts that it had once because it thinks it is clever to attach "that" thought to "this" event. The Angel of Love cannot analyse, it has no brain. It just is.

Comparators:

When we judge one thing against another we are using comparators. These are often non-specific, in that we do not state what we are comparing with, such as "I think it is better like that"; better than what?

When we compare one thing against another, one person against another we may believe that we have the power to make an accurate comparison. However, is it really benefiting us? Why should we judge one against another? Why should we feel we have to be better than another? We are all unique and valuable, we are not less valuable because another person has value too.

The Angel of Love cannot compare:

The Angel of Love exists only at this moment. Therefore all comparison is pointless. It has no store to draw upon. The Angel of Love cannot compare because it sees all things, all experiences and all people as valuable.

Persecution and Damning:

When we determine that something a person has done makes them bad for all time, or that we are "unable to forgive him or her" we are damning.

When we take this further and ridicule, blame, torment, point the finger, yell at or criticise we are persecuting.

Persecution is not a supportive process, we do not feel that we are learning joyfully when we are being persecuted, we feel that we are being harangued. We feel inadequate or angry and want to aggress in return.

Criticism:

Criticism is never helpful. Do not be fooled, even spoken with a silver tongue, criticism is hurtful. Vampires like to use criticism. Sometimes it feels justified at the time, and we listen and nod. Then later we feel uncomfortable and upset by it. We do not need to criticise. So let's stop now.

The Angel of Love cannot persecute, damn or criticise:

The Angel of Love is love. Love is kind. Love cannot be unsupportive.

Catastrophising:

When we catastrophise we take an event and blow it out of all proportion. "It was truly terribly, absolutely awful, just dreadful." Is it really that bad? Of course catastrophes do happen, but is it really a catastrophe when your friend fails to turn up for lunch. Is it such as catastrophe when your child spills the milk? And really, is it so bad when your partner forgets Valentine's Day! In the House of Horrors the answer is usually "Yes, it jolly well is." In the Sunshine of Joy the response is, well, try this one out for size: Do you really need a single day a year to say "I love you"? Is that all love is about? Are you setting your partner up to fail?

The Angel of Love does not catastrophise:

The Angel of Love floats through our world, it exudes warmth, peace and love. It is there, floating. Whatever happens, it is just the same. It does not react; it remains in a place of warmth, peace and love.

The Angel of Love does not get stuck in the past, does not have fixed responses, and does not remember events so that they can be brought up again later. It exists, floats through life, exuding its warmth, peace and love.

Prejudice:

What! Me? Prejudiced? Never! Its funny how we all deny that we are prejudiced, but that when you speak to people from many different walks of life many of them have experienced prejudice of one form or another.

Are you prejudiced? Well first we need to consider what we mean by prejudice. Michael Calwell, in his essay "A Man's Guide to Being Short" clarifies the dictionary definition as ".. a preconceived and irrational judgement about someone's qualities".

Do you make judgements about people because they are: Black/Asian/gay/women/men/fat/short/old/young/redheads/rich/poor/ members of a certain religion, etc. etc."

The Angel of Love is not prejudiced:

As the Angel of Love only lives within the now moment it does not allow cultural factors or peer groups, past experiences of any other external factor to influence it. It therefore is accepting of everything and everyone as they are. The Angel of Love works on the basis that everything is neither good nor bad, it just *is*. In other words, it accepts nature as it is without judgement.

This means to awaken the Angel of Love we need to let go of all our prejudices and prejudgements.

Sarcasm:

Sarcasm is the enemy of all angels. When we use sarcasm we are employing aggressive behaviour that is undermining our relationships. We may have become lost in a world where sarcasm is considered wit. This is not true; wit does not have to be cruel, whereas sarcasm is always cruel; moreover it is usually denied. Most of the arguments that go on between people are due to misunderstanding and denial. In other words, we choose sarcasm as a means of making our point, and then deny that we were being aggressive or unkind. Ho hum. It is incredibly draining. Ban sarcasm from your life if you want to awaken your angels.

Why do we use vampiric behaviours?

When we criticise, use sarcasm, judge, blame, or generalise, it is evidence of our low self-esteem. If we love ourselves we do not need to attack others in this way. When we use any of these behaviours it is an opportunity for us to look within and ask ourselves "What is it within me that has a problem here? Why is this event or person bringing up these behaviours in me?" This is part of taking responsibility.

When we begin to ask these questions, fully accepting that it is ourselves and not the other person who has the issue, we can begin to change and our angel's halo starts to glow.

How do we become angels?

In order to shine up that halo we need to consider how we communicate and use the following simple process. By owning our feelings, rather than blaming others we can communicate our feelings angelically. We can do this by simply altering the way we structure our sentences. When we say "You did so and so" we are blaming, whereas when we say "I feel," we are taking responsibility for our feelings.

However, watch out for the Queen of Hearts, because although we may communicate our feelings, we cannot expect others to alter their beliefs in order to do things our way. When we have transmitted our feelings we may have to accept the way people are, and instead of trying to fix them, concentrate on trying to fix ourselves!

Recognising Separation and Unity:

When we notice vampires we are in separation, we separate ourselves from the world, we see it as a them and us situation. When we appreciate that all is unity, then we also appreciate that to criticise one is to criticise the whole. The taste of the cake depends upon the entirety of the ingredients, not just the icing, not just the cherries in the sponge, it is the whole experience and all the ingredients that make it good to eat.

When we are in unity we accept our role in the relationship, and therefore our role in the successes and problems. We cannot heap blame upon another because we are separating ourselves from him or her.

When we point out the vampire in others we are immediately in separation because we do not see ourselves in the scenario, we see ourselves as separate. However, when we see the Vampire in ourselves as well as in others, then we are beginning to be in unity with them.

We can be in more than one place at the same time:

Can you believe that scientists have proven that the above statement is true! It feels almost impossible, doesn't it? But the quantum physicist can prove to you that your car keys are both under the newspaper and in the drawer at the same time, it is just when you open the drawer or lift up the paper that they will decide where they are! I know this sounds completely bizarre, but there is a truth here, and it is relevant to the Angel of Love.

Once it was believed that things could not be in more than one place at the same time. But is this true? I know I can be in two places at once, and it can be quite confusing! For example, I can be writing at my computer and having a conversation with my husband at the same time. I feel very much as though I am in two different spaces.

In fact we are all living this on a day-to-day basis. As you read this you are capable of a myriad of different emotions and reactions. You may be feeling some right now. You could feel excited, inspired and positive, or you could feel angry, mistrustful and cheated. Whichever emotion you choose to feel (and it is your choice) it is like selecting one pathway from many. All those options are available, and you choose one or two.

Getting into a different dimension:

Take this example, you are going to meet a friend, but your friend is not going to be there, because she has forgotten the date. At this moment you do not know that your friend will stand you up, so you are awash with different possible emotions and reactions to what will happen. Perhaps you could feel angry, or worried about her, or not care and decide to go shopping alone. As soon as you are aware of her mistake, then you will react.

But let's suppose you decide to alter this pattern. Instead of taking the predicted route, you select a new, different, out-of-character choice. It is still you making that choice, and reacting, and feeling. But it is a different outcome. You have altered your world; you are in a different dimension!

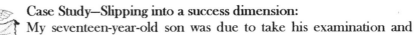

Case Study—Slipping into a success dimension:
My seventeen-year-old son was due to take his examination and was concerned about which questions would be in the exam paper. When he opened the paper on the day of the exam he knew he would be faced with either a difficult or an easy question.

Which would it be? Well, it did not really matter because his response would be to say "Oh great! This question is going to be brilliant and I am going to be able provide an exceptional answer." He would slip into a success dimension.

Unifying all the pushes and pulls:

The world is full of forces that attract and repel, and relationships are no different. All these different forces hold the universe together, and our energies hold our relationships together. Part of this process involves the push and pull of the energies. There maybe times when I exert a pull on your energies, and when you exert a pull on mine. This is all positive and healthy. Part of having a relationship is to be able to share the universe's most precious and yet most freely available commodity; love.

When we are able to give and receive appropriately we feel our relationships as rewarding and energising. Even though I know my vampire has sometimes risen, I can quickly antidote it by awakening the angel and gaining the energy I need by fair means *and not* foul.

My partner does not resent my pull on his or her energies, because it is a mutual process, and he or she knows that I will soon be reciprocating.

Real Relationship Magic or Alchemy:

The magic of the Angel of Love is SYNERGY. When we get the balance in our relationships absolutely right we experience this. Some people may say it is the feeling of true love, but this is to romanticise something that can equally happen in friendships, with work colleagues, our parents or our children.

Synergy is a natural phenomenon. It is the moment when both people feel that in giving energy to the other, freely and in a balanced way, they are actually receiving more back. In simple terms, it is $1 + 1 = 3$. It is a magic formula; it is alchemy. In other words, we are creating something from nothing!

Changing your world:

Lets get back to our example of the friend who has let us down. What will we do? In one dimension we may get so angry we break off the friendship, in another we may rush around and try to find out what is wrong, in another we may not care a hoot, in another we may call her and have a good laugh about it. Which one will reinforce the relationship? Which would give us the greatest satisfaction in the long run? Which one would help our angels to thrive?

This is how the world is changed; how your world is changed. Moment by moment. Living as one in unity, seeing us all as one and the same. "The injury I cause you I do to myself". Yes we can change, we can be the person we dream of being, because that person already exists—it's true, and if you like things to be proven then remember the scientists have said it. If you like the idea of magic then remember, this has been the spiritual truth of many different religions over the years since the beginning of man and womankind.

The Message is Love:

Love is the answer: love yourself, because otherwise you do not allow your love to be a part of the whole. Unify in love, not in lack of self worth.

If you are to love the world then make sure the vessel in which you keep your love is treasured; treasure you, for you are that vessel.

If you are to receive love from the world, open your heart to the love that pours from every part of the universe, love and connect lovingly with all and everything. Make sure you are worthy of that love, and to do that is simple. Value yourself.

What is the price of gold?

Who determines the price of gold? Its price is determined by how much we value it. If it is rare we may value it more, but in fact, it is because it is beautiful that we really give it its high value.

Who determines the value of you? You do. You are not simply rare, you are unique, a one off. The value you give to you is how much you are worth, and every human being is priceless. You too are priceless. You too caused great celebration when you were born; you were priceless then and still are.

And even if you feel you were not the subject of celebration on your birth, know that, when you look up to the stars in the sky and as you feel the earth as it revolves around our sun, we human beings are a part of the grand scheme of life, and that we cannot fail but contribute to it, because we are each wholly and completely unique, and therefore no one but you can be you.

And you have work to do here.

Every possibility already exists:

There are infinite dimensions in which you already exist at this very moment. Which will you choose here and now? Every possibility already exists. Slip into your joyful, loving and fulfilled dimension and be there now—its up to you—it takes no more than a simple thought. Sow the seeds of love in your mind.

Summary

We need to stop trying to fix others and concentrate upon fixing ourselves.

We must keep our hearts open and alive, even when dealt a blow in love.

Filter your words through the halo so that we take responsibility for what we say and do, and do not blame and judge others.

Love yourself, and you will give the universe, your relationships and your God their greatest gift.

MOSAIC Approach:	Examples:
Mission What do I want to achieve?	To know that all people are part of a whole, and lovingly to act from this knowledge that "as I look at you, I see me".
Opportunity for improvement identified What areas in my life could do with improvement and change?	I am very critical of other people, often unnecessarily, because it makes me feel superior.
Skills and abilities are assessed What am I able to do, what will require practise?	I realise that criticism of another is really criticism of myself and low self esteem. I need to apply this knowledge and alter my behaviours accordingly.
Atmosphere is assessed What are things like around me? How supportive are family/friends/colleagues?	I feel insecure so I must ensure I affirm regularly to improve my self-worth everyday: "I value and love myself"
Impact of changes are considered Will there be problems, if so what are they likely to be and can I deal with them?	I may forget to do my affirmations and fall back into bad habits.
Catalyst What can I do to speed changes into place? What will work as a catalyst for me?	Keep a notebook of my new habits and tick off every time I follow them. Reward myself for successfully employing the new habits.

"Change Thinking" Assignments ✓

Think about filtering your words through the halo, even in retrospect; think about how you could have used angelic communication and learn from the experience.	
Do not assume that if you suffer a blow in love that it is the end of the world.	
Life is not good or bad, it is not just or unfair, it just is. Imagine a tree, it is neither good nor bad. Notice if you impose expectations upon life and try to avoid doing this to reduce disappointment.	
Waking Mantra:	
I love myself, and in loving myself I recognise that I am part of the unity of man and womankind.	

"Take Action" Assignments ✓

Identify the habits you want to alter or create.	
Make a notebook or use your diary to list these and tick them every time you follow them through.	
At the end of each week reward yourself if you have carried out 80% or more.	
Keep open and trusting, use your intuition or instincts and go with them when they tell you there is danger.	
Explore life as neither good nor bad. Every time something happens say "that's interesting.." rather than judge it as good or bad.	

Endnote:

Finally, call *all* your angels into full wakefulness:

I awaken the Angel of Joy
I choose to live in a joyful world

I awaken the Angel of Passion
I yield to my passion, I love my vibrancy, I am energised by my belief.

I awaken the Angel of Freedom
I fly above my fears, I am the authentic me

I awaken the Angel of Courage
I shine in my brilliance

I awaken the Angel of Truth
I am secure in stating my needs and allowing them to be satisfied

I awaken the Angel of Love
I love and accept myself, I am gentle and kind with myself and the world with whom I am in unity.

Make good angelic magic,
and electrify the universe with your love!

References and recommended further reading or viewing:

Author	Title	ISBN	Notes:
Adams, Patch	Gesundheit	0-89281781-8	The Red Nosed Doctor's philosophy on life
Berne, Eric	Games People Play	0-14-002768-8	Manipulation in relationships
Canfield, Hansen, Hewitt,	The Power of Focus	1-55874-758-4	Find your brilliance and shine
Choun, Marcus	Cycles of Creation	New Scientist	Is the universe stuck in an endless loop of death / rebirth.
Covey, Stephen R.	The 7 Habits of Highly Effective People	0-684-85839-8	Excellent text for making changes in your life.
De Bono, Edward	Lateral Thinking for management	0-14-013780-7	Creativity at work
De Becker, Gavin	The Gift of Fear	0440226198	Survival Signals that protect us from violence
Foundation for Inner Peace	A Course in Miracles	0-670-86975-9	Personal and spiritual growth.
Gibran, Kahlil	The Prophet	434-29067-X	Beautiful, meaningful and relevant today.
Goleman, Daniel	Working with Emotional Intelligence	0-7475-4384-4	Bringing heart and mind to work
Hay, Louise, L	You Can Heal Your Life	1-870845-01-3	How to love yourself and right your world.
Holden, Robert	Happiness Now!	0340713697	Tapes and books to raise a smile and welcome you to joy.
Hoff, Benjamin	The Tao of Pooh	0-416-19511-3	Simplified teachings from the East; flow and acceptance.
Hort, Barbara E.	Unholy Hungers	1-57062-181-0	Encountering the Psychic Vampire in Ourselves and Others
Jeffers, Susan	Feel the Fear and Do it Anyway	0099741008	Finding inner courage
Joseph, Sandra (Edited by)	A Voice for the Child - The Inspirational Words of Janusz Korczak	0-7225-3806-5	Discover angel wings by understanding children.
Laborde, Genie Z.	Influencing with Integrity	1-899836-012	Communication skills that do not abuse power.
Maslow, A. H.	Motivation and Personality	006049873	
Miln Smith, David Leicester, Sandra	Hug the Monster	0712670165	Seeing the child beneath the vampire's mask.
Pinkola Estes, Clarissa	Women who run with the wolves	071267134x	Finding personal freedom
Renshaw, Ben	Together, but something missing	0091855934	Relationship expert, Ben, provides invaluable advice
Spezzano, Chuck	If it hurts, it isn't love	0340818646	A guru speaks!
Peat, F David	Blackfoot Physics	1-85702-456-7	Native American Insights
Williams, Nick	The work we were born to do	1-86204-5526	Joy and meaning in our work
Williamson, Marianne	A Return to Love	0722532997	Finding your inner light
Zukav, Gary	The Seat of the Soul	0-7126-4674-4	For real growth and insight

Fictional references, biography -recommended further reading or viewing:

Author	Title	ISBN	Notes:
Carroll, Lewis	Alice's Adventures in Wonderland	0140620869	The Queen of Hearts
Dunmore, Helen	Your Blue Eyed Boy	0-14-027217-8	Examples of fictional Needy Vampires
Eggers, Dave	A Heartbreaking Work of Staggering Genius	0-330-48455-9	Biography - witty and full of pathos, a demonstration of real self awareness and love
Grisham, John	The Firm	0099830000	Nests of vampires
King, Stephen	Salem's Lot	0450031063	Searching for vampires and finding them! Lots of vampire myth.
Lewis, C.S.	The Magicians Nephew	0-020442300	Insights into science and spiritu-ality.
Millman, Dan	Way of the Peaceful Warrior	0-915811-00-6	Self awareness, understanding how to find the gifts and go with the flow.
Rice, Anne	Interview with the Vampire	0708860737	The trap of vampirism - interest-ing vampire relationships.
Stoker, Bram	Dracula	014062063x	The original work.
Strieber, Whitley	The Hunger	0688037577	The attraction of the vampire
Suess, Dr.	Oh, The places you'll go!	0-001712-66-7	Sound advice that should be taken by adults!
Suess, Dr.	How the Grinch Stole Christmas	0001700154	Learning to be more giving and accepting, and finding that we can increase our joy.
Walker, Alexander	Audrey, Her Real Story (Biography of Audrey Hepburn)	1-85797-352-6	Inspiring biography of a woman who gave much to humanity

Film	Year Released	Studio
Dracula	1931	Universal
Wall Street	1987	20th Century Fox
Interview with the Vampire	1994	Geffin/Warner
Tootsie	1982	Columbia
Working Girl	1988	20th Century Fox
Blood for Dracula	1974	CC-Champion & I
The Firm	1993	Paramount/Mirage
Patch Adams	1998	Touchstone
The Ice storm	1997	Touchstone
The Lost Boys	1987	Warner
The Hunger	1983	MGM/United Artists
Alice in Wonderland	1951	Disney
Roman Holiday	1953	Paramount
Nosferatu	1922	Parano
Dance of the Vampires	1968	MGM

Angelic Relationships:
One Day Workshop conducted by Maria Paviour

Now you can bring your friends, family and work colleagues together to benefit from this exciting and entertaining workshop.

Your will learn how to:
- Create a balance in your life and work
- Draw love into your life
- Shine in your brilliance
- Develop rewarding relationships at home and at work

Human Synergy Coaching
Working with individuals, partners, families.

Become a high achiever, discover sources of untapped potential and find out how to live life to the fullest. The Human Synergy Coaching Programme is guaranteed to change your life for the better. Don't let fear or finance stop you. Talk to us, we can help you today.

Phone now for information:

International +44 (0) 1825 830370
UK 01825 830370
Email: Isiliver@btconnect.com

Synergy Training
Creating Synergy in Human Relationships at Work

WellBeing@Work™
Improving Employee Effectiveness and Morale

Maria and Stuart Paviour and their team of licensed consultants can help your organisation to develop effective employees who contribute to bottom line success.

This proven system:
- **Creates a high, measurable return on investment**
- Enhances effectiveness
- Reduces distractions and errors
- Increases focus

For further information on how you can improve *your* profits through the Wellbeing@Work™ system
please call now 8am to 6pm week days:

International +44 (0) 1825 830221
UK 01825 830221
Email: info@synergytraining.co.uk
Web site: synergytraining.co.uk

If you are interested in becoming a licensed Human Synergy consultant please call the above number for information.